My  Codex

Volume One

The stories behind the most famous historic mysteries and treasures

Brandon Curtis

MYTHIC CODEX

Copyright © 2022 by Brandon Curtis.

All rights reserved. Printed in the United Kingdom. No part of this book may be used or reproduced in any manner whatsoever without written permission except in the case of brief quotations em- bodied in critical articles or reviews.

First Edition: July 2022

Contents

Mythic Codex 1

Contents 3

The Lost Dutchman's Mine 4

El Dorado 78

Wonders Of The Ancient World 103

Easter Island 121

About the Author 136

The Lost Dutchman's Mine

The Superstition mountains in Arizona holds over five hundred years of history around a lost treasure. The range the mountains cover includes the Superstition Mountain itself, with the surrounding peaks and canyons for miles around. Across this wilderness suspicious and frequent deaths guard the truth. At the heart of its legend is a treasure, rich and exploited throughout the centuries. The ownership changed many times to those daring enough to venture out to regions protected by the Apache, keeping knowledge of the mountain's wealth hidden, only known to those who had found it before. From the stories left behind from those who found it, it is one of the richest gold deposits in the world. Ever since it was last found the truth became the legend of the lost Dutchman's gold mine.

Forty miles east of Phoenix are the edges of the mountains. Since 1872 this 4000-foot-high peak has been adeptly named the Superstition mountains from its lore. The area is covered with rolling hills of rough red and brown rock. sharp peaks as far as the eye can see, filled below with rocky canyons in the valleys. Low lying bushes with dry wood grow all over, covering the hillsides and colouring the land with their yellow flowers. Vegetation in this rocky area makes travel exceedingly difficult being so thick and jagged. One wrong step has on numerous times caused unfortunate travellers their lives.

Trails through the valleys guide travellers over the land, the rest of the place is over rock and thick plant cover. Shade is hard to come by with few trees being able to grow in the dry heat, there only a few areas which can support trees, at the bottom of some valleys there is enough ground water for cottonwoods to grow. Aside from the few trees, cactus grow all over thriving with the lack of water. Air around the valleys is hot and dry during the day, tiring the fittest of people. Overnight it cools rapidly, making this exposing land unforgiving to the elements, by those unfamiliar with the area.

Indigenous Tribes
500BC-1450

Indigenous peoples have for thousands of years settled the area, from those who were knowledgeable enough to make the environment hospitable. The Hohokam, a native American tribe were first to settle Phoenix. They dug out hundreds of miles of irrigation trenches, directing water across plains allowing land to be cultivated. These first people to have permanently habited the area eventually vanished, thought to be from droughts draining the river and becoming unable to support themselves had to leave.

Once the land permitted a return, it was home to the Pima tribe. Living in the Southwest of the mountains, along the Gila River. They were the descendants of the Hohokam; gaining their name from Conquistadors who met the tribe on their exploration. When they tried to communicate using Spanish, the onlookers repeatedly said 'Pima.' For them it translated as 'I don't know,' not being able to understand what was being said. They were primarily farmers living off the river they stayed by. The collective was made from two neighbouring tribes, they are distinct having their own cultures and traditions but are close allies through their many shared values. A union was to the benefit of groups making a single power, each with their own respective leader. There ancestor tribe had a large stone-built settlements, after their environmental collapse could no longer keep building and maintain large structures so abandoned them in favour of village life with more primitive housing which the Pima kept practicing.

Apache territory was to the North of the superstitions. They were a warrior tribe, again not a singly body of people, but a collection of culturally similar groups, using the same language and shared customs across Southwest America. They were a native hunting and gathering society, some being nomadic following buffalo migrations and living in tepees, which could be easily dismantled and moved to follow the heard. Other tribes led a more agricultural life having a permanent residence. Each elected their leaders democratically by their social standing. On occasion they would clash with the Pimas on hunting trips in the shared superstitions.

Wars fought for years because of the Apache ferocity and unwillingness to leave their native land. They fought both Mexicans and Americans for decades, before the creation of reservations. Even then, after they were granted assurances, they would still come out from the reservations, during the spring and summer months, forming war bands and raiding parties. They would take horses and guns if they did not illegally trade for these prized possessions. They successfully raised the horses they acquired, riding them from an early age becoming proficient.

The largest mountain in the range, is on the Western boarder of the superstitions. Named crooked-top mountain by native Pima; it bursts out the ground with steep incline from volcanic activity. It is around this mountain where the most gripping tale of a treasure takes place. Large enough to draw anyone to join the hunt for the lost mine and various gold caches left by careful miners in their hiding spots.

The New World
1492 – 1519

Stories of the riches coming back from the New World, soon accumulated after Columbus returned with tales of his discovery. It encouraged further missions to travel there and return home wealthy. Europeans launched many campaigns. Most were successful the most devastating was made by Hernan Cortez and his army of just four hundred Spaniards. As their ships appeared off coast, natives had no way to describe the Spanish galleons, floating islands was the most appropriate to describe this new construction, carrying on their back's the new travellers.

The natives were quick to side with the Spanish, impressed at their vastly different appearance, with clothes and technologies including cannon fire, the sound it made was terrifying the earth would shake and violently explode around natives charging to the Spanish, halting in fear. The Aztecs of the Americas were living in relative peace with their environment, but not as well with independent neighbouring tribes. They would launch war campaigns to take further territories, making alliances with other powerful tribes that agreed with them or conquered by them.

1521

Siding with the Spanish brought the collapse of the Americas, not knowing that outcome at the time it was deemed the best course of action. The Spanish and native coalition army, toppled the capital of the Aztec empire Tenochtitlan, imprisoned and killed their emperor. Rebuilt the Aztec capital birthing Mexico City, which attracted new settlers. Gold was found to be in the possession of natives all over the empire. Their artifacts were melted down and sent back in ships to Spain. A substantial portion of the emperors ransom never arrived before his execution, leading to tales that it was redirected, hidden out of reach.

1540

Cabeza De Vaca, was an explorer coming over to America. Along with his crew they became shipwrecked along the coast of Texas. They had to journey on foot to

Mexico City over the mainland. They arrived with tales of finding Cibola, the mythical seven cities of gold. Soon stories of Cibola were waiting to be discovered, drew expeditions past central America travelling further north. The Spanish arrived to the area of Phoenix, led by Francisco Vasquez De Coronado to search for the cities. It was there they met the Pima's; they seen their jewellery and had asked where the source of where this metal came from, they replied by pointing to the mountains.

The Superstition mountains were first referred to, as the mountains of foam. High up near the peak a white limestone line is near the mountains crest said to be the remnants of an ancient flood. Before the Spanish got to explore the region, they met with the Apache. They believed the mountain should not be entered; it was home to their thunder god. He lived in caves and would sleep irregularly to deter anyone from suspecting any safe moment. They would make a sacrifice of an animal to appease the God and be allowed passage only granted to the natives who would hunt deer, chasing them mountain ridges and follow them down into the valleys.

Undishearten by tales of vengeful pagan gods, the Spanish ventured into the mountains unphased. As soon as their expedition began, members of the party started to vanish in moments they were away from the rest of the group. They were usually found a few days later, often missing their heads. They quickly left the area, naming it 'Monte Superstition'. After numerous other searches were made, no cities of gold were ever found. The search expanded settlements across the area and filled in blank spaces of the maps after going these new regions. By 1590, settlements had created areas made suitably for metallurgy, bringing the tools they needed into Northern Mexico.

Jesuit Priests
1609

Though land was now becoming settled, it was not safe from the natives, who knew their land far better than those from the East. Making stealing their prized possessions like cattle and horses easy using guerrilla attacks, striking quick and fleeing. The Peralta family name first makes its first mark on the land here in Mexico at this time. Pedro De Peralta, was named governor of New Mexico and commissioned to establish settlements more impervious to Indian attacks. Shortly after new towns were built and missionaries were sent in, bringing religious teachings and converting natives.

These missionaries consisted of catholic priests named Jesuits. They reached the Gila River, seeing silver jewellery in the Pima's possession. Like to explorers before them, asked where it had come from, the friendly tribe pointed to the source of this material being in the superstitions. As new conversions to Christianity, they were enlisted to mine the source of this metal and it would be sent back to Spain. They opened several mines in the mountains, above the workings lay a large heart shaped rock with a quartz 'X' and a crack on the front. As work continued mines were made deeper and expanded to make several tunnels.

1701

A Jesuit named Father Kino was successful at teaching and converting locals. He was building a cattle ranch reaching as far North as the Superstitions. While on his travels he would create maps, he was trained as a cartographer and accompanied over two dozen church missions into Arizona, as a representative of the church. He would conduct ceremonies and church related business establishing holy sites. He taught Indigenous people's Eastern techniques for farming and introduced European crops for the natives to experiment growing and brought cattle to the land. It is said he came across a rich gold mine, which added to his influence in the area. He was later joined at his settlement by other priests, who enslaved natives to work farming fields and in the mines.

1751

Infrequent missions ventured into the Superstitions, the journey there and working out in the mountains was dangerous from the Apache threat. Mining in their sacred mountain was a major insult, taking away resources of the thunder God. Gold had been the cause of driving the new settlers mad with greed, always leading to the persecution of the natives. Decades of enslavement and poor treatment ended with a revolt, where the Jesuits are killed and natives abandoned the mines. Over a decade later in 1763, new missionaries had arrived who had considerable success with conversion elsewhere in the Americas, were sent to Gila. By then trust in the settlers had long diminished and Apache's raiding was making life insecure, it did not permit mining to be re-established.

The Peralta's
1768

The Peralta family were still wealthy and influential in the region. Around this time the church offered to the family the location of the Jesuit mine, as well as a portion of the wealth coming from the mine which would fund fighting the Apache, they would keep a third of the mines wealth while giving the rest to the church. The Peralta's accepted the terms and employed men, they bought the relevant supplies and set out shortly after to locate the mines.

They came across the Pimas and managed to build a symbiotic relationship with them. By allowing them access to the area of the mountains, they would also be providing protection for the Pima's from clashing with the Apache. The Peralta's continued past the Pima settlements, up into the mountains. After a brief time, they managed to locate the heart shape rock at the top of the cliff face above the mine. Underneath they found the tunnels at the base of the cliff, they reopened the tunnels and began mining them periodically.

1797

After three decades of mining and ranching, the Peralta's business exploits had made them wealthy, they had contributed to a considerable amount development to towns. Mining was only done on and off with its dangers. They found there was plenty of money to be made from cattle ranching and trading livestock, which was far more rewarding. With ranching all the profits belonged to them, while the church was taking two thirds of their mined material. Trading routes were built over the Superstitions for livestock to be transported and sold. Trails wore into the land over years after herding hundreds of animals through the tracks. Along the way through the mountains the animals needed water, there was not enough for amount of cattle they were wealthy enough to bring through. They built walls and basins along the path to hold water in the bottom of canyons. Although there are springs throughout some valley floors, they are unreliable. You would need to know their location and then hope the source still existed or any you would be caught in trouble.

1828

Along one of the many journey bringing livestock through the mountain, they had stopped off to take a break to drink from one of the springs at the bottom of a canyon. While collecting water while looking down into the creek something glistened under the water's surface, golds was discovered laying at the bottom of the riverbed. The creek was prospected to find the source of gold coming from a nearby mountain. Gold pans were taken further up the creek, the further they travelled, more gold was being collected in their pans. Leading up the creek they finally found to the source of gold, which had made its way from the mountain side down below.

The gold existed in a layer of rose gold quartz, hidden in between narrow canyon walls. Across the other side on the canyon was a natural cave which overlooked the valley below, it was ideal for a look out point. Inside the cave was tall enough the stand up in and contained a small source of water to the back of it. If any Apache did manage to find them hidden out there, they would surely avoid being ambushed and the cave could make an ideal defensive site. Using what little trees existed in the area, they built a defensive fort inside the cave. It overlooked down to the mine entrance and across the canyon floor.

Below the cave on the opposite side of the valley wall was the location of the pit mine. It was following an 18-inch stream of the gold rose quartz. It was incredibly rich for any operational mine, the ore of higher quality than found before. As the pit mine reached deeper the tunnel started to show signs it could cave in, fearing the worst they dug a secondary tunnel. They started it a few meters above the first in the side of the sloping canyon wall, tunnelling down until they connected to the main pit and continued mining further in.

1847

A considerable land grant gave 3750 square miles of Arizona to Don Miguel Peralta. He built more silver and gold mines in the Superstitions. The Peralta stones were maps leading to mines, they are carved into rock and left at the side of the trails to guide expeditions. The legitimacy of the Peralta stones comes into question as the centre of a hoax from James Reavis. A soldier in the confederate army, who would forge military documents for his friends and those who offered to pay him. Most confederate documents were handwritten which suited Reavis as he had a skill for forging names. When it became apparent the South were losing towards the end of the American civil war, he moved over to the union army. He was caught forging documents but was recognised for his calligraphy talents. He managed to get a job making copies of documents in an archive, he used this to change documents concerning land grants. Making a trip to Spain, he took with him his forged land grants giving him land in Phoenix. After the American civil war, land grants that were made pre-war would be honoured.

One of the Peralta stones happens to be marked with the date 1847. It could be the case Reavis used the stones to legitimize his fake land claim existing pre-war. He was paid tax by the mining companies on his false claim. When some of the larger mines recognised the claim others followed.

The stones could otherwise be a legitimate product from the time of the Peralta's, marking in secret the route to their mining locations.

1846 – 1848

The American Mexican war had just begun. When American forces approached Mexican towns to take their land. The Mexican government spread word about the brutality of the Americans, hoping to cause outrage and start an uprising against the invaders. It only served to terrify Mexicans who instead fled terrified.

Before the impending war, the Peralta's had moved into the mountains. Living by their mine which they had named Sombrero mine, to continue mining as much gold as they could before the area was taken. Over the course of the next few years, they opened and excavating new mines as the war went on. Before the end it was becoming clear the Americans would win. After their victory they would gain a lot of the land in the area. With fear of being discovered if the soldiers of the Apache arrived and weighted down by the ore they had collected, they decided to deposit some of the gold at the bottom of dug out cisterns. They were built to function as a basin, catching and storing water for the miners. They left knowing it would be kept safe over summer if anyone travelled to the area. They gathered as much gold as they could take with them. Concealed the entrance to the mine, disguising any trace that mining had taken place in the area, and began the slow decent out of the mountains.

During the war, the Apache were equally feeling military pressures. The tensions pushed them further into the wilderness of superstitions. With the mine work finished as the Peralta's attempted to leave, they were noticed bringing gold away from the sacred mountain, which caused outrage. Gathering all their numbers, they ambushed the Mexicans. Gold was being carried in saddlebags on the backs of burrows, when the Apache descended out the hills and fighting broke out, the burrows ran scattering most of the gold they were carrying. They were killed and were left where they lay, their contents intact. The area this attack took place is known as massacre grounds as the miners were trapped. During the attack all but two of the Mexicans were killed, two boys survived by hiding in thick bushes, one of which is Don Miguel Peralta. Either escaping by remaining undetected until the Apache had moved on, or left by their mercy. They managed to survive and headed back to Mexico carrying the tale. The story stuck with Don Miguel who would remember the mountain well.

Over the next decade, prospectors in the area reported finding and collecting piles of spilt gold ore, found near the skeletons of several dead burrows, their saddle bags still attached. The ore contained $37,000 ($2.7 million today) of gold. The land of the Superstitions and its surrounding area was granted to the Americans after the war. It was soon after settled creating Phoenix after twenty years. The area was still a dry and parts desert, but it contained plenty of land for farming and a good climate for crops. The original irrigation trenches created thousands of years ago by first natives to the area still existed. They were expanded with new channels dug to improve the areas water supply to help the towns growth.

1864

The Peralta family did not head back to the mine for some time. Eventually Enrico Peralta took four hundred men back into the mountain. Mining had always worked best with small parties to best evade detection. This time he took four hundred men, for one last trip. The large expedition was soon noticed. The Apache attacked, coming from a North-western slope. All the men including Enrico were killed in the ambush. The lure of gold was no worth the risk with the Apache concentrated in the region, now fully aware of their trips. The mine would lay dormant for the time being.

Simon Novinger
1867

One of the first tales of gold laying to be claimed in the Superstitions, reached American settlers a few years after the Peralta miners had ceased work. On the field surrounding Phoenix, there was a farmer raising hay named Simon Novinger. One day during the summer, he was visited on his farm from an American boy, roughly 14 years of age. His English was poor and could barely communicate at all, he was skilled riding on horseback, so allowed to stay on the farm to work for food and a place to live.

Just before a year of his employment had passed, his English was improving enough for him to begin to communicate with Simon. He said he had lived with his family in Texas before an Indian attack came to his village. His family had not survived the attack, being so young the Indians took him in their tribe to be raised by them. Over the next decade he was passed around a few various tribes, eventually living with the Apache in Arizona.

When he was fourteen, they decided to let him go back to his own people. They took him towards American settlements and let him go back by himself. From there he walked through ranches and farms, looking for someone to take him in. No one would want to take him in with his lack of English, soon after he found refuge on Simon farm. During his time helping around the farm, he accompanied Simon and seen the sale of hay they had been working hard to raise, it was being traded for a small amount of gold. The boy was surprized that so much work could be worth so little. He had realized the value given to this material by Americans.

He excitedly told Simon of two sources for this metal he knew about from his time living with the Apache Indians. They only valued gold for its spiritual purpose unlike the American. He knew of natural gold deposits which had been worked by the Apache on a small scale. With their experience from the Spanish and the Jesuit priests, they knew the invaders were driven mad by the substance, while the Apache protected it for its natural value as part of the land.

The gold sites the boy knew of were both in Arizona. The first was part of an old riverbed, having long ago been raised from geological forces hundreds of feet high. It left deposits on the river bed, freely scattered on the ground which could be picked up. The site was named 'rich hill', it was recently discovered by Americans and is thought to be the source of native American gold, as it was available without being mined. The other site was near a peaked landmark in the mountains nearby, it was a mine which contained much more gold.

The peak said to be a marking location is weaver's needle. Pauline Weaver was a known explorer in the area, who would trapping animals and prospect throughout Arizona in the early to mid-1800's. On a large peak central in the Superstitions, seen from far around, he engraved his name in the rock. It was later being discovered by prospectors, since it had been referred to as Weaver's needle.

Simon Novinger had experience in mining early from his working days. He did not find enough to hit a big gold rush; it was more of a dream than a profession. Now hearing tales of a location, kept secret by the natives where gold waiting to be claimed, sparked the interest of Simon. By now the boy had been working a year, he had previously agreed to be paid with a horse, at the end of a year's work. Now knowing the wealth he could access, he asked if he could get his horse early to set out and find the mine. Simon cautioned him not to leave straight away, but to wait until the cooler winter months before travelling into the wilderness. This would be when water and food were most available for himself and his horse to make the journey.

By this time a year has passed and the boy had grown. He may not be recognised or known to the natives if he passed them. At this point they would surely be hostile towards him, so going alone was a huge risk. This was unknown to the boy having been raised by the Indians, to him they were his friends. So, he left Novinger's farm, travelling on his horse towards the Superstitions, he would never be heard from again.

1968

The next again year, over the cooler winter months. Simon, along with a small group of friends, travelled out to Arizona to find the raised riverbed with gold easy to pick at Rich Hill. When they arrived the area, the land had already been divided into allotments by prospectors making it their first, who had control over the best claims. They settled for a claim, managing to pull a moderate amount of gold out of the ground. It was not enough to satisfy the tales of vast riches that was expected.

The group became divided between the contentment of the modest amount of gold they could get from Rich Hill. Or leave going after the far larger deposit at the mine, which they would have all the access too. There were two peaks of recognition in the superstitions considered after being mentioned by the boy being near the mine. First the peak most associated with the tale being weavers' needle, second is sombrero butte. Simon travelled with one of other party members to look for the lost mine. They went to sombrero butte, after searching they could not find a mine location but would continue, beginning what came to be a lifelong passion of exploring the mountains always looking out for the hidden entrance.

Doctor Thorne
1865

In the years since the Peralta massacre, the natives who fought the miners had left most of the ore on the ground where it lay. They had filled some back into the tunnel it had come from and cover the entrance over. The remaining scattered gold waited until the first time an American came to the mine, his name was Abraham Thorne. After finishing medical school, he needed job experience, deciding the best place would be out West, he moved to the frontier where he was able to travel and find plenty of work to practice his skills as the most conflict was out West.

Military camps were built on the frontier, the doctor travelled through a few camps before he came to and stayed at Fort McDowell. He worked to help both the American soldiers and the Apache, providing much needed experience for him. While in contact with the Indians curing them of their ills, he gave more for than just medical care. During time of war for the Apache living their nomadic way of life must have been under tremendous pressures. The outside world continually surrounding them, which enviably conflicted with their way of life. The morale of the citizens would be low at this time, by tending to their wounds and curing them of diseases from a trained doctor. Giving care to them worked to psychologically uplift their spirits.

Over time is presence became welcomed by the native people. He grew close with them working for years out in the dry heat. After he felt he had enough experience, it had become time to move away back to larger towns and build his own practice. After telling the Apache of his soon departure, the chief who appreciated the doctor as he had cured him. Asked if he could return to the Apache camp the next again day, one final time to receive their thanks for all his work. He was to be offered a reward.

Doctor Thorne set out from Fort McDowell and travelled to the Apache village; he was met from a band of friends coming out from the village. Before they set out the doctor was blindfolded, they set out for the journey without him being able to see his route. He was hesitant before making the trip, they were coming into the hot and dry summer months. At this time a trip into the mountains would come with risks, if water was not found the springs dried up, the Apache would sacrifice their horses first. The doctor would not be so easy to go through with it and figured the trip would not be advised.

Nevertheless, he was assured there would be plenty of hay for the horses and springs to drink from. They set off at night-time, during the trek the Indians would try to disorientate and confuse the Doctor, to hide the location of their journey. They would cross the same bridge multiple times and double back on themselves along the route. Doctor Thorne was able to keep his positioning through these attempts to conceal where they were going. He could hear children talking who were accompanying them and the sounds of the nearby spring, which kept him focused.

By daybreak they had arrived in a canyon, after what he estimated to be a twenty-mile journey. They stopped and dismounted their horses, being relieved of his blindfold the doctor looked around the canyon. He could see a sharp peak to the Southwest, no more than a few kilometres away. Across at the opposite end of the canyon, laying further North he could see four peaks from hills.

Laying out on the ground, by the side of the canyon wall was a pile of rich gold ore. The Apache instructed the doctor could take as much as he could carry, which he did. He then had his blindfold tied back on for the trip back. After he returned to the village, he departed from his friends and made his way back to the military base. He confided in one friend to what had happened to him during his time away. He gave a piece of gold to his friend and went on to travel to New Mexico with his ore, he was unsure of its value but was grateful to having received it.

On the way to New Mexico, four companions accompanied him. Along the road they were attacked by a band of Apache warriors, two of the men were killed immediately. The attack was about to have killed all the men, who could only hold the Apache off briefly with slow rifle fire. Without four men shooting they were closing in. A voice shouted for the attack to halt, one of the members of the warriors had recognised the doctor. He was well known, being the white man who tending the wounded and became well respected for it. He had been a member of the Arizona Apache, apologised for the ambush and offered the doctor and his surviving companion two horses. They were escorted to the Pima villages before giving the horses back and continued that last part of the journey to New Mexico by themselves. When they had arrived, he brought his sack of ore to the assaying office, where he sold it for $6000 ($200,000 today).

Although he was not permitted to see or explore the mine, he had only seen the area where the gold was, believed it to be close to its entrance. He was not allowed to ask questions of its origin; he was just led to the ore stacked against the canyon wall, that remained after the

Peralta massacre. It had since been collected and left in piles.

1869

The story Doctor Thorne confided to a friend had started to spread. Stirring the imagination of those who heard it, the story soon became Doctor Thorne's lost mine. Those seeking adventure and treasure would attempt to relocate the area described for years to come. Searches would set off from Fort McDowell, moving into Apache territory the entourage would often encounter hostile Indians, who would deter them from travelling further across their land. It was not worth starting a confrontation over so many turned back. One group did manage to get down past the Salt River, going through the superstitions to look for the mine. They did not come across any canyon containing gold along its walls like the doctor description and disbanded. It was not to deter one man amongst the party, he decided to continue his search on his own. He became integral to the history of the mountain, after all the mine is named after him. He is the dutchman himself Jacob Waltz.

Jacob Waltz
1810 – 1891

Born Jakob Walz, he was raised in Germany. Growing up he worked as part the family business in cloth making, though he hoped not to stay wanting to travel. When he was thirty-one, he emigrated to the US where he changed his name to Jacob Waltz. There are many variations of that Waltz story, each portraying him quite different but all equally having him with a vital role in the legend.

Two of these opposing stories stand out. The first, and by far the more credible of the two, is most referred to being the real the story behind Jacob and his hidden mine coming from Reinhardt Petrasch. He was a boy who lived in Phoenix at the time Waltz stayed there. Reiny's family, whose surname was Thomas became close friends to him in his later years. Waltz told his story to Reiny, who later relayed the tale after his death. The second account of the Dutchman story comes from Dick Holmes. Quite differing, it portrays Waltz as a violent killer, his ruthlessness kept his mine secret by killing anyone who stood in the way of his treasure. Dick had met Waltz in the mountains, like most people living in Phoenix, knew of the rumours surrounding Waltz.

While both stories are as equally intriguing, part of the legends and can become mixed through the many versions told. Reinhardt knew Waltz personally, he had become close to the Thomas family for a while and though he was a secretive man, there was less of a reason to distort the facts to those he did trust. If he really was a ruthless killer in the mountains, it does not fit to his character for many of the stories surrounding him. It is easy to accuse Waltz as responsible for all the misfortunes to come to travellers entering the wilderness. The most reliable source of information would therefore be coming directly from Waltz telling it himself to Reinhardt and his mother Julia Thomas.

The Petrasch version of Waltz

It began while Waltz was serving in the confederate army during the civil war. Over his time serving in the military, he claimed he never killed anyone. He left soon after the war ended, his ability to speak German and English suited to clerical work post war. It was during his work here; he met his friend named Jacob Weiser. After a few years working together, Waltz heard tales of gold rushes across America. Those who got there first would make quick fortunes, which attracted him to start prospecting through Arizona.

He was always behind after gold rushes; areas would be quickly claimed with frenzies of treasure hunters flocking after gold was found. Being too late he continued moving from town to town. For a time, he worked at various mines, one being the Vulture mine learning how to work a mine. For those working for someone else, wages were not particularly rewarding. Still, it gave it him the necessary skills he needed. He left after being suspected of high grading ore, low wages could be subsidised by keeping the best pieces of gold found for himself. Though he was never caught he was suspected of it. At the beginning of the civil war in 1862 gold was found in the Gila River, with the threat from the Apache it was too great a risk to get much exploration around the area until after the war had finished.

1870

After a time of prospecting and moving around Arizona, Waltz settled in the Salt River valley. He bought a plot of land where he raised hay, he was able to employ Mexican farm hands to help tend his fields. He still had the interest and excitement for the adventure of prospecting, so would continue whenever he had time. By the end of the year Waltz along with his friend

Weiser, had travelled to Sonora Mexico to try their luck. They had stopped off in a saloon where they were enjoying a drink and looking over to a card game when an argument broke out around a table. Two men had a disagreement over the game, the dealer continually won and was now being accused of cheating. Taking such offense to this accusation, 'being outraged he was caught', stood up and stabbed the man in the shoulder with a knife.

Onlooking as the confrontation unfolded, Weiser immediately ran over took out his pistol and hit the dealer over the head with the grip knocking his unconscious. The second man who had been stabbed was tended to, he was grateful for the immediate reaction of Weiser, helping him without any hesitation. The three men began to talk, Waltz and Weiser digressed their intentions in the area being prospectors looking to hit it big. The man was interested in their story and seen the whole event as a sign. He was Don Miguel Peralta, hearing the men were miners and now knowing they were tough. He told them that he was in possession of a rich mine, granted to his family by the church. He was in the stages of planning one of the infrequent Peralta trips back to the mine, to reinstate the family's wealth as it had been wearing away.

Being grateful for having his life saved his life, he offered the two Germans along to accompany him and his team of labours. Offering to pay the men fifty percent of the ore taken as a reward for the bar fight, for providing protection along the route and staying to oversee the mining. The men agreed and soon after set off into the mountains together with Don Miguel and his team of miners. Once they were deep into the mountains they had arrived at a narrow canyon, they spotted the cave used by the Jesuits, previously as a look out point. They rebuilt it to be a suitable fort and used the freshwater pooling in the back of the cave. Across from the cave was an entrance leading to the inside of a pit mine, it had a narrow opening by the base of the canyon wall, like a funnel going deep underground.

Inside of the tunnel, wooden shelves made of mesquite wood that had been cut around bluff spring mountains, ran along the walls. Wooden beams to support the inside structure were squared around the inside. To climb in and out of the entrance there was a wooden post, made of cotton wood with notches carved into it, it would help miners grip onto when they were climbing in and out of the pit with ore. Down the canyon from the mine was a source of water, close enough to access but a fair enough walk away it was not quick to get to. They spent several weeks opening and excavating the mine, while the labourers done most of the groundwork the Germans helped coordinate the process.

The gold stream running through the mine was vast. Waltz claimed there was enough to make twenty men millionaires. Gold in that day was worth a whole lot less than it is today, converting it over time, twenty million dollars back then would be over one billion today. After weeks of work, they had finished. The readied to leave, loading up all they could carry on the back of burrows. They travelled out of the mountains with Don Miguel and the rest of the group.

When the Germans were about to head back to Phoenix, Don Miguel was saddened by the men's departure. They both had rifles and were good enough shots to deter any Apache band they may still come across them on the way home, he had hoped both men would return with him to Sonora. Don Miguel was a most persuasive man and convinced them to all travel back together. When they made it back, Don Miguel talked of the debts he owed. After the trip they had 30,000 dollars' worth of ore (2.25 million today). With half belonging to both Waltz and Weiser they had made their fortune. Don Miguel was about to strike a deal with the men they could not refuse. He was more interested in paying off his debts than risking more trips back up to the area. He asked if the Germans would leave their half with him. In return they would be allowed to claim the mine and work it for themselves for as long as they want. The men accepted, they received a map drawn cow hide, serving as a reminder to the mines location and went about planning the next trip, this time to make their own fortune.

On the trip back to the Peralta mine, Waltz and Weiser managed to easily enough find their way back to the narrow canyon and to the location of the mine. It was late in the afternoon by the time they arrived. At the base of the canyon floor, they managed to collect what little wood they could gather, to build a pen for the burrows. It backed against a large boulder and needed two fences with a large log acting as the gate at the front. This would keep the animals safe from wondering away, if they were spotted the Apache would soon follow them and find the men working the mine. They also functioned as an alarm;

they would alert the men sleeping in the cave above the canyon, if anyone was approaching them and startled the animals. They would begin excavating work in the morning, they climbed up the side of the canyon to the cave entrance, staying inside the stone house looking down on the entrance.

During the night Waltz woke to the sound of tapping coming from across the canyon. It was the late hours of the night and far too dark to see clearly. He could just hear the distinct tapping of metal against rock, someone down below was trying to reopen the mine. Waltz woke Weiser and the pair picked up their rifles and readied them, they were not about to lose their secret mine so quickly. They left the cave and silently crept back down the canyon and hid between thick low-lying bushes.

As they crawled closer to the mines entrance, they came close enough to make out the silhouettes of two individuals. They were quickly working picking away at a spot above the mine entrance, the Germans though they were digging in the wrong spot as it was so dark. They did not want them to stay overnight as the cave was the obvious refuse. As they dug and uncovered rock from the slope, stone rolled down the canyon, falling around the pit entrance.

Waltz and Weiser had figured the pair were Apache warriors. They had known about the mine after the battles with the Peralta's and two of them had now come up to mine it themselves. Not being able to share the mine with any Apache, they took aim and shot both men. They returned quickly to their cave in case any other

Indians, which there would surely be other within hearing distance, would have heard the gunfire echoing across the valley. They would be quick to send out a search party.

Over the rest of the night no one came, the men had elected to stay up in turns to keep a look out. The echo from the shot hid the precise location of the gunfire, which was heard in the nearby Apache villages, they sent out search parties but found nothing. By morning, the men left the cave and headed back down from the cave to the mine entrance. They were horrified reaching the mine to see the bodies of two men. They were not Apache but Mexican labourers, they had been a part of Don Miguel Peralta's workers they had just arrived back with to Sonora with. They must have figured they could sneak back up to make a quick fortune for themselves, trying to beat the Germans back to the mine making it in the dead of night for a quick haul. Considering it was so infrequently worked and with no mention from Don Miguel of sending another trip so soon, they had not thought of the men being Mexican, making them out to be Indian. Realizing their mistake, they were in shock, neither had ever killed anyone before. With the gold in reach and the sudden awakening that a hostile Apache was right by them, made them think taking the shot was the best course of action and regretted it ever since.

They looked at the rock removed by the Mexicans. What they had removed revealed a secondary shaft, found above the first and travelled downwards to connect with the pit below. That morning they buried the men and began mining down in the secondary well-hidden entrance. Underground they collected plenty of gold together and hauled it up to the surface. Over the next few days, they created two small caches of gold hidden nearby somewhere in the canyon floor, in a spot only they could find it, they then hid one final large cache of gold. It would secure some gold in case anyone else claimed the mine. Spending their time collecting gold now would mean next time they came, as they had far too much to carry back by themselves and their burrows, would not have to stay long they could just collect their gold.

After a few days of working had gone by, they came down from the cave one morning to notice one of the burrows had escaped out from the pen at night. It had walked over to the nearby supply of flour bags they needed for the trip, which was kept hanging off tree branches. The burrow had burst into the bag and had eaten through a lot of their supplies spilling each bag. Instead of cutting their trip short and going home, the men agreed that Waltz would return to town, get more supplies and come back to extend their trip. Weiser would stay behind and continue working the mine and store more gold.

Waltz travelled into town, taking with him some of the gold they had collected. He was expected to be away for three days. His trip was held up needing to replace one of his horses' shoes holding the trip up by an extra day as the blacksmith was away until the next again morning. Waltz returned late on the third day he found the camp abandoned, he shouted on Weiser he heard nothing back. The pen was destroyed, the animals and Weiser missing, presumed dead from a sudden Apache raid. Waltz blamed himself for his friend and partners death which always stuck with him, he gathered one of the small caches and returned to town.

On the morning of the Apache attack, back in the camp Weiser was expecting Waltz to have returned by now, Indians came out from the canyon to the north. A flying arrow found its way into Weiser's shoulder, he knew he was in trouble. Getting to his horse, he rode away stopping off to occasionally to keep the ensuing Apache band back with rifle fire. The chase went on for hours through the hot sun. Weiser's condition from his injury had been worsening throughout the day, he managed to make it to a spring. He stayed only long enough for a quick drink, unaware if he was still being chased or how far they were behind him.

His horse had died from exhaustion on the way back being pushed so hard in the heat. He had to leave his rifle behind, its weight was slowing him down too much. Leaving it could prove to be equally damning. He managed to make it out of the mountains and reach to a Pima village. He was brought to a doctor's house, from an examination his wounds looked bad, signs of infection were setting in and it was a huge concern.

His doctor kept him company for the night and Weiser told his story of how he ended this way. When his infection began to take hold the next again day, it became evident that his recovery was not going to happen, it was only a matter of time before he died. He decided to show the doctor the Peralta rawhide map he and Waltz had received. He said he and his partner had received permission to work the Peralta mine. Now that his partner was surely dead, being due back early on the third day and not making it back when expected just before the Apache attack, Waltz was thought to have been surely found and killed first, leading the Apache to the mine for Weiser next. Now both men were going to die, Weiser thought it best to tell the doctor so he may find it for himself. He died on the fourth day in the doctor's care. Unbeknownst to Weiser, Waltz had only been delayed which had saved his life, showing up to the camp just hours after.

1873 – 1878

Waltz was put off from going back to his newly acquired mine, he refrained from going back for blaming himself being the cause of Weiser's death and they had killed the Mexicans. Soon after the temptation would draw him back travelling to the Superstitions, this time with just himself and his burrow. Military roads had since been established round the mountains, which cleared away a lot of the Apache threat. Not that the danger no longer existed, just lessened from the nearby presence of the army.

Waltz was gone for weeks at a time, armed with his rifle for his safety against bandits, Indians and now ever suspicious he was being followed from town into the mountains. Rumours were spread around Phoenix of how rich his gold was. One day after a few trips to the mountain he came back into town to resupply, his burrow ladened with rich gold. He would buy mining equipment and supplies for his trips paying in ore, which was common for the time. It was the richest rose gold quartz that anyone had seen before, leading to the naming the mine after him as the Dutchman. Jacob being German, is said to have preferred conversing in his native tongue, he would stay quiet when hearing Americans speaking English. If they asked where he was from, he would reply Deichmann meaning German, this would be mistaken for Dutchman, thinking he is from the Netherlands.

He would not say where his gold came from, nor did he ever file for a mining claim granting him rights to the source of it. He did not make many trips to the mountains over the years just going to collect the caches they had left and mine a bit when he could. On his final trip to the mine, he concealed the entrance over with rock then putting bushes over.

1881

Jacob continued living in Phoenix after his last trip to the mountain. Over the years he seen the town grow, starting small in its early days. It was no bigger than a village when Waltz arrived building up his farm and prospecting through the area. The town had a population no larger than 250, it did not have access to the railroad until it grew large enough over the years. It continued to attract settlers reaching 2500 citizens.

1884

One of these new residents was Julia Thomas who moved with her family. She was a married woman who had two boys, one of which Reinhardt Petrasch. Like the dutchman he was also of German descent. Jacob enjoyed being able to converse using his native tongue, he befriended the boy along with Helena. He still worked on his farm and would bring over extra eggs when he had some spare for the family. Helena opened a bakery and sold confectionary, with poor business management she had bought an expensive piece of equipment and now she could not make back loan repayments. She would give out tabs to the children visiting the store, inevitably they ever paid back the money which risked Helena bankruptcy.

Without anywhere else to turn she confided in Waltz to being in considerable debt and about to lose her business, upset with the situation she put herself in. Waltz considered their friendship, he did not want to see the family move town, so offered to do whatever he could to help her out financially. He asked Julia to send Reiny by Waltz's home later that evening. Now ageing he would need help from the boy to travel to Julia's house.

That evening Reiny showed as promised to Jacob's home, entering he found Waltz gathering tin cans together on his table. Their pair loaded up cans inside the burrows saddle bags and they set off walking across town to Julia's house. When they arrived, Reiny helped Waltz carry in the heavy tins bringing them inside. There Waltz opened one can and brought out some rose quartz, showing Julia the gold inside. He instructed her to write to the bank, confirming her debts would be paid fully very soon from a friend resolving the finances. Waltz had experience selling gold, he knew it would take a few weeks to claim money from the transaction of selling the ore after it had been sent away to be smelted. The whole business would have to be kept quiet to protect himself. He would refuse to give her the money she needed, which was around 1200 dollars, if she did not keep quiet as he did not wish word to further spreading around town and wanted his gold had to be secret kept.

1890

A few months later on in the summer, Waltz had invited Julia and Reiny over one evening to have dinner outside with him in the sun. As the evening went by, Jacob had been behaving unusually being quiet, thinking to himself for most of the night. Towards the end of the evening, he had finally decided what he wanted to say. He began by confiding to the pair there was more gold than what he had given the family from the cans. That he had knowledge of a gold mine, where they could get all the money they would ever need, though it was in rough and dangerous country. He began to tell the story of his adventures, how he had acquired the mine and continued to travel there over the years. By now he had removed the second small cache over the years. He was now too old to mine any more, Helena and Reiny did not know how to mine but the last remaining large cache of gold ore was still hidden and needed to be brought back and in the cooler winter months. He decided they shall all make the trip together.

1891

Before winter came, Phoenix had suffered a huge flood which washed away a lot of the town. Waltz was caught in the flood; he was stuck inside his submerged house for a few days. When it was safe Reiny was able to stop by and check on him. By that time Waltz was suffering from pneumonia, an illness from which he would not recover. He was brought round to live with Julia and Reiny, over the next few months he often thought he was going to get better. At least recover enough to make it part of the way into the mountains, when it got too rough, he would have to stop and would give them directions to find the mine.

He never did recover enough to take them and died that October. Over his last few days, he told Reiny he had a chest buried under his fireplace. He hoped it remained intact after the flooding and asked if he could take it out for him. Reiny dug under the foundation of the fireplace, found the chest and put it under Waltz bed at Julia's house. Fearing the worst, he tried to explain the best he could the location of the mine. Along with his description he noted multiple times Reiny was not paying close enough attention, he would need to know exactly where it was to find it. It had been covered up last time Waltz was there, even standing just a few feet away the entrance it would be unrecognisable. Among his descriptions of the area, he stated from the mine location he could see Weaver's needle; he could also see the military trail but from the trail you could not see the mine. During mid-afternoon, the shadow cast down from Weaver's needle would shine into the mines entrance. In Waltz's last moments he needed a doctor, Helena left him to fetch help, when she had returned with a doctor,

Waltz had died. The chest under his bed was now gone and was never recovered.

1892

In the weeks that followed Helena sold her business, thinking her troubles were all over once they reached the mine. Her and Reiny set off at the start of the year. They looked for many weeks before the search fell apart. Arguments started with frustration as Reiny was not paying close enough attention to the directions, soon after he abandoned the search. Although they never found it themselves, after Waltz's last trip to the mine in 1978 and at the time of his death, there was an earthquake in the 1887 which affected the area around Arizona and the Superstitions. The fall out may have had drastic changes in the landscape, explaining their lack of success even with Jacob's description.

The story spread around town and across the state that Julia Thomas now searching for the Dutchman's mine. Treasure hunters were attracted to the area, being a part of the legend Helena was a person of interest. She produced and sold her own maps, leading those who would pay the equivalent of a few days' wages, to get for themselves the clues to the treasure. Looking at the maps she drew, Helena had made them up, they contain no truthful information. She sold a few over the years, each seems to drastically change. If she really did have any idea where it was, she would have found it herself. Reinhardt had moved away after giving up the search, sometime later he was found dead, with a shotgun wound to the head. Possibly being held up for information about the mine.

Two soldiers
1880

Over the time Waltz worked his secret mine, there are others claiming to have come across hidden gold after trips into the mountains who came across a hidden mine. Two unnamed soldiers, having left Fort McDowell decided they wanted the adventure of learning to become cowboys. They saved up all their pay from the army. Unlike everyone else, instead of using some of their wages to pay for transport to town of Pinal, they decided they would save money by walking and camping along the route.

On the way they entered the Superstitions, they spotted a deer on a ridge above them. They shot at it, chasing it over the top of a ridge and down into a canyon below. When they had caught up to the wounded deer, looking around they noticed evidence of occupation in this remote area, finding scattered rock left over from mining. They soon found a tunnel, kneeling and looking inside it was entrance to a mine. The adventure of mining filled their excitement, even better than being cowboys. They collected as much loose ore as possible from inside the pit. They were unsure what kind of ore they possessed and would have to get it checked out and headed the rest of the way to town.

They arrived at Pinal, where they immediately went about finding work. They offered their services to Aaron

Mason, a mill owner who was also had a silver mine. They enquired about the ore they had found and talked about the mine they had come across. They described it as being to the North of a sharp peak in the roughest country, Mason identified this as Weaver's needle. Mason was curious about the ore; they were exceptionally good specimens. He agreed to have the ore assayed for its estimated value which Mason would pay the fair value to the boys.

It was estimated being worth $700 dollars ($52,000 today). The soldiers were shocked to hear of its value. They claimed there was lots more where that came from, they had only taken away a fraction of it. Now abandoning the idea of becoming cowboys, the attraction of mining offered to pay more instantly became more alluring. Mason advised they should be silent about their discovery. They should buy supplies carefully from around town and head back to get what more they could find. Mason had not heard of such a mine in the Superstitions, it was an area he was familiar with and refuted its existence. He thought they came across it and took everything there was, not leaving behind much more much. If a mine did exist it was surely abandoned, the ore would have been almost depleted or with altercations with the Apache the value of gold left in the mine was not worth going back for.

After deliberation between the boys, they decided to spend the money they received from the ore. Along with what they said saved from the army, to buy rifles, pistols, horses, and mining equipment. They will go back and collect more to bring to Aaron. They had at least two hundred dollars left over between themselves after buying all their equipment. They had left some with Aaron who would hold onto it until they got back. They were sure they could rediscover the mine, on the journey to town they regularly turned around, seeing the direction they came from in the opposite direction, to be able to retrace their steps to find the mine again.

They claimed there was so much more, they asked if Aaron would become a partner of theirs and share in this mines wealth as he was far for experienced in the business. He agreed if they could go out and collect more as proof there was a mine. He would then be convinced to visit the mine for himself, if it is as valuable as they claim he would send the men and resources needed for the job.

He encouraged the boys should file the correct legal claims and gain permits to the mine and he would help them doing so when they returned. With that the boys were ready, they both set off for what was to be a four-day journey. Two weeks had passed, no word had come from the boys. A search party of twenty men was sent out to look for them, setting out from Pinal. After a few days of searching found nothing, looking in the direction they had travelled. They eventually came across two bodies when the search widened. They found them undressed and mutilated, having died from bullet wounds. There was a military hat nearby which identified the pair. They were buried where they lay, the deaths initially looked like an Apache attack after what they found, leaving a body nude and mutilated was common for them. It was not until later a suspect came about, the towns people think the murder was disguised to look like an Apache attack, after shooting the boys to conceal suspicion of an American as the killer.

In Pinal at the time, there was a man working in the local saloon. He would only do simple jobs around the hotel; his job was referred to as being a swamper. He done what he could cleaning the latrine and tidying up. It was a job usually reserved for older men, the work was simple and less labour intensive than other work. This man was younger, the reason he could not do a more demanding job, was he suffered from a twisted foot.

The swamper would often sit in the saloon, watching card games being played. He would often ask for a coin from a lucky player so he could play himself, much to the disgust of the dealers. He never had any luck and was soon enough back asking for handouts. One day he left town for a few weeks without a word of where he was going. When he returned, he had a lot of money to spare. He made several extravagant purchases and started to gamble with his own money, to the surprise of all the locals who all revered him as a moocher. When asked about his new wealth he claimed he went to Florence and there went on a winning streak making all his money.

Soon after his arrival with his wealth, word began to spread about the recent finding of the two soldiers' bodies and their connection to a secret mine now reaching town. It was the topic of discussion all over, someone jokingly said to the swamper in the saloon, he must have been the killer, taking his wealth from the two soldiers and their mine. He shrugged the comment off, but the idea began to resonate with the people of Pinal, soon suspicion started to grow. It had been known that the boys had purchased mining equipment in a small town where word quickly spread. The towns people gathered, the swamper could have heard these rumours of the boys mine, presented himself as a partner to the soldiers. He could provide some help labouring as well as protection in the dangerous country or looking after the animals brought with them. While on the journey to the mine or more likely on the way back after learning its location, he could have taken the soldiers rifles at an opportune moment, turning it against them both. There clothes could have been burned low down in a nearby canyon the smoke being undetected, their horses quickly killed too making them unidentifiable and taking the remaining money they had on their person, as well as the location of the mine. All the while removing all suspicions of himself by disguising the killing as just another Indian attack.

After he was further questioned about the truth behind his money, he responded angrily feeling it was right to be questioning a man's wealth and was outraged at being scrutinised over it. The citizens of Pinal, decided it they would need to make an enquiry about the legitimacy of his newfound wealth. A local businessman was about to travel to Florence, he was asked to make enquiries about the man with the twisted foot, having been there and going on his winning streak.

During the enquiry in Florence, stagecoach drivers were questioned but no one had taken any man fitting the description. Neither had any gamblers frequenting the saloons had seen a man with a twisted foot. It raised suspicions further to where his money had come from and why lie about its origins. When the information from the enquiry made its way back to Pinal, it was enough to convince the town he had to be hiding something. The towns folk met to discuss what should be done, with emotions raised several members of the group argued the swamper should be hanged for what he had done. Other members were against this, it was unlawful to accuse a man of murder with no questionable evidence. They settled with the excommunication of the swamper because the days of public executions had gone. When the appointed member of the town, selected to inform the swamper of their decision to kick him out tried to find him. He had left his residence and had already gone.

Joe Derring
1881

Word of the two soldiers' deaths was spreading across the state, where it reached Joe Derring. He had spent time prospecting across Arizona, but like others before him never having any luck finding enough gold to make it past a recreational hobby. Captivated by the story of the two soldiers who went walking through the mountains, stumbled across the gold mine, making themselves rich. Joe was the very first man to go out specially searching for a lost mine.

By this time, a year had passed since the soldier were killed. Joe went exploring out into the mountains, closely following the story of the soldiers. He went North from Weaver's needle, then passed into a narrow canyon where he came across a partially blocked tunnel. He was surprized to have stumbled across it so easily, though he had found his mine and achieved his goal, he was now stuck with a secret. He had no knowledge of how to mine the ore and no funds for the equipment he would need either.

He decided it would be best if he got a job as a miner. He would work long enough to be able to buy the equipment he needed to excavate the tunnel and would learn how to go about working inside. He travelled into Arizona and asked about getting a job working at the Silver King mine. The management of the mine was currently away for the following week and would not be able to be hired until the owners return. Not being the type to sit about town waiting, Joe enquired if he could help out in the saloon until the mine owners return. He was big and built up so was hired to sort out any trouble from the customers. Although he had no experience with mixing drinks, he could pour them straight, as long as he was keeping busy and able to save a little bit of money it was worth it the weeks work.

Derring became friendly with the saloon owner over the next few days. He became open to tell him the story of the mine he had found. Describing the location as being a ghostly place, in the roughest terrain you could find, he was saving to work it for himself. He described the mine itself and a funnel shape pit, with a large opening at the surface which went down underground. At the time he was there, the entrance was partially obscured being filled in.

Inside the pit there was a walled-up entrance leading into the tunnel itself. It was joined from above by a secondary shaft coming downwards. From his brief time there, he had brought back pieces of loose gold ore he could find and carry back with him. He found some laying in a small pile by the side of the mine entrance. Looking down the canyon it was recognisable being narrow compared to the rest, finding it again should not be a problem. Once the mine owner had returned a week later, Joe asked and was given a job working at the Silver King. During his first week working, Joe was caught in a cave in, a shaft which he was working in collapsed crushing his leg, he died from his injuries soon after keeping the location a secret.

Novinger's later search
1881

Simon Novinger had continually kept going back exploring in the Superstitions, often travelling to Sombrero Butte, in search for the lost mine the boy had brought to his attention fourteen years earlier. On one of his trips, he was travelling back to the mountains with a few men, when they were ambushed. The Apache were hiding in the mountains and shot down at them with guns and arrows. They were able to keep them back a while, holding them where they were with rifle fire, the Indians kept their distance.

Simon grew frustrated at shooting the Apache from the back of his horse. It was too unstable to take a clear shot and he continually missed hitting his target. He climbed down from his horse to gain a steadier shot. While climbing down he tripped, stumbling on his foot hold, he dropped his rifle. It went off exploding as it hit the ground, flying shrapnel from the shot hit him and caused severe injury to his leg.

Realizing they were being chased off the land and neither side hoping for a fight to the death. They managed to keep the Indians back long enough with consistent gun fire to get away. They gave up advancing on them, allowing there to retreat to Fort McDowell. Simon spent the next four months there recovering from the disaster. Even after receiving medical treatment and recovering, he could never walk the same again. It prevented further ventures into the mountains for the treasured mine. Though was no longer able to go himself he kept the story.

Years later years Jim Bark, a rancher and Dutch hunter, who built the bark ranch at the western edge of the Superstitions and met with Simon Novinger. He told Jim his stories from travels looking for the lost mine. Jim went on to research and look for the mine himself. From what Simon had said, he was searching around Sombrero Butte the whole time. After hearing the story, Jim considered Sombrero Butte not to be the correct peak in reference to the boy's story. The peak was instead was Weaver's needle, ever since it has been primary peak marker for the gold trail.

Doctor Thorne returns
1883

As the years moved on, since Doctor Thorne had left his time around Fort McDowell. He had been running a successful doctors practice. He did not keep all his wealth given to him from Apache to himself. He continued to care both Americans and natives, if a native needed his medical attention or required antidotes but could not pay. He used his own money to buy it for them, becoming again well respected in his new community.

Eventually as years passed, he began to think more about his adventure into the mountains and the strange cache of gold he had seen. Realizing its value after being sold, what else could be in those mountains waiting to be found. He began to question where the source had come from. If he could find his way back to the site, he could find the mine entrance if it was in the same canyon with the scattered gold he was brought to. From his generous charities he gave in his medical practice, he was steadily spending through his money and eventually the wealth diminished.

Over time he had told his story to close family members. They were amazed by the adventure and tried encouraging Doctor Thorne to go back into the mountain, where they could all go looking for the treasure. He always turned down the idea as it was dangerous and he was always contempt with what he had received. Now he had spent through his money, he eventually he accepted the call back to the mountains and went about finding an expert.

He told his story to Robert Groom; he was prominent in the business and familiar with the mining industry. He told about the sharp peak laying a few miles, no more than six, to the Southwest of the canyon he was in and set out with a team of eight to Pinal, where they would begin the journey. They left late in the year, avoiding the worst of the summer's heat and they would find the most amount of water for the journey. They travelled to Weaver's needle, from there went between five and six miles past, travelling Northeast where they made it to a canyon. There lay an old fortification built up the side of one of the valley walls. He was sure this was around the location of the ore deposit, looking around they did not find any trace of gold on the ground. The team searched around the area for any sign of a mine entrance and were unsuccessful. After a short stay revealed nothing, they gave up and returned home. It is possible that from the last time Waltz was there at the mine, he had left it covered over. Joe Derring later also stated it was partially covered over, which could have been further buried in the two years since Joe had been there. It was said by Waltz himself, even near the mine even just meters away, it would remain undetected. Finding it would require knowing its exact location. The mine was never claimed to have been located since.

The Hermit of the Superstitions
1896

Elisha Reavis, known as the hermit of the Superstitions, was a schoolteacher in Illinois. He was compelled to move to California to search for gold, being unsuccessful and left and went back to school teaching in Arizona, still prospecting on the side. Again, unlucky searching for gold he moved back to California after a few years. He started a family and continued life in California for a while, he left them and took off four years later. Heading back towards Arizona he made it to the area around Fort McDowell. With his family connections living in the area, he managed to get a job as a deputy marshal for the territory of the Superstitions. After four years of working as deputy, he decided he had enough and left his life behind to live in the mountains by himself. He became as the madman living in the hills.

A story of his character demonstrates his compassion and attitude for the natives around him. One day an Indian peacefully walked by his house, Reavis immediately took out his gun shot and killed him, leaving the body where it fell. A couple of days had gone by, the Indians friends were concerned about disappearance from the Indian village and went out searching for him. One member of the search went by the Reavis ranch, where he was shot and killed too, also being left on the ground by his friend. The Indians caught word of the further disappearance by the ranch. They organized a large party to come by his house and surrounded the place.

Reavis was in the middle of a stand off by himself. He shot out the windows at the Indians until he ran out of bullets. The shooting had taken so long, the sun had fallen. Now as darkness was setting in, finally able to overpower Reavis as he could no longer use his weapon. They instead decided to stop, it was a tradition of the Apache not to fight in the dark. They left, to resume the attack in the morning. They sat a bit away from the ranch, lit campfires and waiting for the sun to rise and signal the destruction of the house and to kill the man in retaliation for their own losses.

Reavis was not prepared to wait so long, under the cover of darkness he left his house. He came over to the campfires to confront the men. When he arrived, he was completely naked and wielding two knifes. He shouting at them and he jumped into their campfire kicking out the hot coals towards them. They were shocked at how crazy this man was. They were a superstitious people, believing a man's craziness is linked to his closeness with his god. They should not kill him as his craziness will pass on to themselves.

They ran away shocked and left him and his ranch alone from then on. He farmed crops for himself and would travel back to town where he would sell his crops around Phoenix. He was known in town, always being scruffy and unshaven. He would take his favourite burrow from the mountains into town to sell what he had left over and resupply before heading back to his ranch. In 1896 he was now getting old; life was getting tougher living by himself being so remote. The few friends he had around town, would occasionally go up to visit him. Reavis had not come into town for a while, they thought it best to check on him. When his friend got to his ranch, he found the body of Reavis decapitated. His head placed on a stone above his body looking down at it, no one was ever suspected of the murder.

Ernest Panknin
1915

Ernest Panknin had just arrived in Arizona; he had moved to help alleviate himself. Suffering from tuberculosis was common, in those days it was believed hot dry air was beneficial to reducing the symptoms. He had long suffered from this affliction and had often moved out to the warm climates of Yuma in Arizona. Once he felt well enough, he had returned to his home in Alaska. This time he needed to return to the dryer climate, had chosen to stay in the Salt River valley, at the edge of the Superstitions.

When he arrived, he intentionally set out to find Dutch hunter Bob Bark. He told Bob he specially travelled to the area. A friend from Alaska had told him a story of a rich gold mine, he said it was the richest gold mine in the world and was sure it still existed. He also knew it to remain undiscovered, its contents are so rich, word of its discovery would have spread all over America. He would have heard about it even in Alaska. He thought others had tried searching for it, but it was difficult to find so no one had come across it.

Ernest asked how his friend knew this and where it was. His friend drew him a map across two pieces of paper, this map marked important locations leading to the location of the mine. Finding these locations led along the trail to the mine and would need to be found. He did not include the mine location on the map, which was to be instead committed to memory. If anyone stole or acquired the directions themselves, they would still not be able to find the entrance. Ernest, enquired to Bob if he could help him identify the landmarks drawn his map. On his way to Phoenix, he had been asking others about the map's locations, a sharp peak and a green spring, others had identified the peak as Weaver's needle, but no one had heard of green springs. He had been encouraged to find Bob, as he was a hunter for the gold and if anyone knew lesser travelled areas up there it would be him.

On Bobs journeys through the area, he had become familiar with many trails leading through the mountains. He quickly identified the sharp peak as Weaver's needle, the springs he said he had never been himself, but knew there used to be a spring which gained that same name. Algae grew in its waters, turning the surface green, but had long been dried up. He had only ever travelled close by but knew at once point it did exist, the mine entrance was Northwest from this spring.

Panknin told Bark about his friend from Alaska, who relayed this story of a lost gold mine. He said they had worked together. He had helped him find his job and when Ernest became ill from his tuberculosis, he was looked after by his friend. After a while in his care had decided it would be better to move back to the hot dry climate, until he could control his symptoms would be best for his health. His friend then asked where he would go, he was surprized as to hear him say Arizona. Ernest explained he had stayed in Yuma before, which had helped him and was considering going back.

His friend wished he could go with him, before moving to Alaska he had lived in Arizona at Pinal. When he stayed there, he had learned the location of this mine. Ernest questioned if his friend was so knowledgeable about this mine's location, why not travel to Arizona himself and claim it. He went quiet and admitted he dare he would never return to Arizona, though he wished he could. Still, he was interested in helping his friend claim the treasure he could not and gave him the map. He explained to Ernest, even if he were to return, he would be too old to working a mine anyway. Least of all, he could not work a labour-intensive job, as he had an affliction from a disability. His friend suffered from a twisted foot. Ernest went on to stay in Phoenix, regularly searching for the mine but could never find its exact location. He wrote back to Alaska asking for further help finding it. When no response came it was apparent his ageing friend had since died.

Dick Holmes version of Waltz
1878 – 1890

The other iteration of the Waltz story comes from Dick Holmes. He had moved out to Phoenix during the years Waltz had returned to the mine, following his partners death. During the time when Waltz made his trips into the mountains, his activity was being noticed by the town's folk, who were talking of this guy's incredibly rich gold. He would come to town with and buy whatever he needed. Word was spreading and Jacob was turning into a local legend.

As Dick Holmes travelled through Arizona, passing through ranches and farms to reach Phoenix. He was passing by a ranch and came across a cowboy sat out by himself round a campfire. He asked if he could join him for a while, the nights were cold and he could use the company. Dick said he was traveling across Arizona looking for work, the two began talking and Dick heard a story coming from Arizona. The cowboy said there is an old man, who guards the secret of a lost mine. He would go into the mountains and return weeks later with considerable amounts of rich gold. He had built himself a large house in town, which even had a lock on his front door. This was very unusual for the time; they were expensive being used commercially and by the wealthy. Yet this old man was able to buy this and felt a need to protect himself and his home. He kept to himself on his farm for the most part but would occasionally sneak out of town. Hidden by nightfall to disguise his direction he was travelling; the town only knew it was in the direction of the Superstitions.

Jacob's story began when one day himself and his partner Jacob Weiser where prospecting through the Superstitions. Travelling eastwards up Queen Creek they entered neighbouring canyons and came across an abandoned camp with an unattended fire, they sat down to recuperate by the fire. After a brief time three Mexicans arrived back to their camp, they were surprized to find their remote camp, being so far in the wilderness was attended. They were happy for the men to stay with them for the night. They said they had been mining close by, the Germans were therefore the same reason and were interested to what the men were mining, they showed a specimen of ore to the men, they were astonished how rich in gold the ore was.

The Mexicans said there was so much gold there, they could all help work the mine together. They would all be able to extract more ore and there was enough to go around between them all. One of the Mexicans knew of the mine from their childhood. He had been a part of an expedition before they were attacked. It was that assault which went on to be known to be the ambush at massacre grounds. Of the two young boys who survived by hiding in bushes, managing to escaped back home to Sonora they had never forgot the location. Don Miguel Peralta was now grown, he had brought two friends back to the mountains and showed them the location. The next again day, the five men set out from the camp to find the mine entrance; it was located a short distance away. The Mexicans were killed in cold blood by Waltz and Weiser to keep the secret location to themselves. Still, it was not enough for Waltz, he then went on to kill his long-time friend Weiser too, securing the mine to himself. By all accounts of how rich the mine was said to be, it seems unlikely greed would take over and feel a need to keep it all for himself. A larger party would be more defensive in hostile land far away from town.

Other versions of how Waltz acquired the mine, tell of how the pair were prospecting through canyons next to the mine. They did not initially spot the mine entrance as it was covered over. Around the valley floor around the site, they found the cisterns dug out from the bedrock, an obvious sign someone had built them. They led along the way to the mine to catch much needed water, when they had stopped off to drink from its source. Looking down they noticed the glistening of gold ore below the water's surface.

They initially worked excavating the bottom of the cisterns, they pulled out all the gold they could. When they recovered everything, they could, they went exploring the area further and stumbled across the mine, then Weiser was killed. How Waltz found it is part of the mystery. He found it, took what he could then concealed the entrance. They were attacked from a band of Apache. Waltz was hit in the shoulder with an arrow. The only means of making a narrow escape was by leaving behind his horse and supplies. The terrain was rough, and they both had to move quickly, Weiser was killed here from the Indian attack leaving Waltz wounded barely making it out.

Over the next few years, he starts making his trips back to mine and is sending gold back to Germany. One day Waltz's nephews show up to America, he had heard the family told stories of the gold Waltz was sending them. He too was drawn to the adventure and set out to find and work with him. Once they had met, Waltz had agreeing they could go and work together. He could be trusted being family and with an extra person, he could helpful with the labouring by hauling rock, even though he had no real mining experience. They set of together to travel up the mountain. At some point on the trip, his nephew made his intention clear he was going to record and reveal the mines' location. They should get legal mineral rights and tell the world the story of this fabulous gold mine.

Waltz did not agree, he was angered and felt a betrayal by not guarding his secret. He killed his nephew, burying him out in the desert in a shallow unmarked grave. Waltz is subsequently the main figure hiding up the mountains guarding his treasure. All those who died along the way after finding the gold were attributed to be victim of Waltz. This includes the two soldiers, who had announced their trip while buying supplies which angered Waltz. He feared they had stumbled across his mine and quickly rushed out to make sure his mine was secure. When he got there, he waited for them to arrive when he killed them both.

Once the story of the Dutchman was finished being told by the cowboy to Dick Holmes on that night by the campfire on the ranch, the story had stuck with him. Dick parted ways the next again day to continue moving to Phoenix. Once he arrived, he was to look for work. On the day of his arrival not long after himself he sat out looking out at the town from the saloon. He saw an old man arriving with a burrow. This old man with his burrow reminded him of the story he had heard a few weeks before. He decided to follow to the old man into a store. He stood behind him and seen was buying supplies and paid with a piece of gold ore. It further rose his suspicions it could be the same person.

He went back to the saloon, where enquired about the old man. By sheer luck his suspicions had been right, the old man had indeed been the source of the tale he had heard. Over Dicks time living in Phoenix, he kept an eye out for Jacob's activity around town. Eventually he had begun to slowly buy supplies around town, surely for his next trip. Dick waited out over the next few nights for Waltz to sneak out quietly. Finally, there was movement through the town. Waltz was leaving to make his trip undetected, Dick left close to an hour's gap before departing himself, setting out to follow his trail.

He followed for a day, until seeing smoke rising from a small campfire in the distance, he knew he was catching up. When he made it over to inspect the campsite, a metallic clicking sound came from behind him. As Dick turned around the old man stood up from behind a bush, he had his rifle ready and pointed straight at Dick. Waltz was not an amateur while making his treks, he had been followed before and had always evaded leading others to his mine. Sometimes he would go as far as to double back on himself and take others to follow wrong trails, taking them all over the mountains to mislead them. Sometimes he would just return to town and wait for things to quieten down before making his next trip. This time he had hidden and waited to confront whoever was following him. He stopped Dick and told him to go back to town, it was not safe to follow him into the mountains and he would surely be killed. In this version of Waltz, he continued to visit his mine in the mountains past 1878, he continued through the 1880's all the way until the floods of Phoenix in 1890.

At the end of Waltz life after the flooding of Phoenix and he was in the care of Julia Thomas. As she went to fetch a doctor for Waltz, he calls for Dick Holmes to come to his bedside. He begins to speak to the Dutchman, where he recounts all the regrets he has made. Most of all killing Weiser and his own nephew along with all the others who stumbled across his mine. He feels too guilty for his actions and asks Dick to take the chest of gold from under his bed. He is to return it to

Germany where it will be given to his nephews' family. After doing this, he may find Waltz's mine and claim it as a reward for himself, Dick he had left by the time Julia returned and Jacob had died.

This version of who Jacob was, is convenient to account for the mysterious deaths in the mountains. There are multiple adventurers who are found with gunshot wounds and brutality killed after entering the Superstitions. It also covers the end of Waltz life, when the gold under his bed goes missing. This version could even hold some truth, the story he told Reinhardt Petrasch could have been changed as he would not want his close friends knowing his true nature of the things he has done. When he recounted his own story directly to Helena and Reiny, he was quiet much of the evening. When it came to telling the end of Weiser, he repeatedly said that he did not kill his partner over again. This is more likely him blaming himself for leaving his partner by returning late, rather than delusions and being a vicious killer.

Dick Holmes story fails to integrate with other sources coming the time. The story itself never came directly from Dick but is told from his son, who was told the story from his father. Its considered Dick put himself in the story with a significant role being closer to Waltz than he ever was, if the two ever met at all. Reinhardt had heard of Dick Holmes story and laughed at it, not thinking it held any value which is in all probability is an accurate evaluation. After Reinhardt left the area and Julia died soon after. Only Dick Holmes was around to become the local expert, who claimed it was passed to him by Waltz himself on his death bed. Keeping Dicks account close to the original story while no one could refute it.

There is another story of Waltz acquiring his mine after being directed to its location from an Indian girl named Ken Tee. The pair had met along Waltz travels as he was prospecting, he married her sometime after. It was forbidden for any Indian to reveal a mines location to a white man, it made them crazy. Tribal traditional healers, who had high social standing engaged in keeping mines secret and acted against natives to prevent white men learning of mines. There are stories from over the years involving the search for the treasure, which included natives in the search party who had befriended Americans. They often reveal they knew of the location to a mine in the superstitions. These stories always end with the natives becoming nervous, they abandon the journey close to the mine's location. They knew it is against the rules and feared they would be killed by the traditional healers. Waltz learning of its location from his wife was seen as a betrayal by Ken Tee to her people. Her tongue was cut out by the Apache, she was left to die in her husband's arms. He then went on to find its location by himself.

Adolph ruth
1931

At the age of sixty, Adolph Ruth was a government employee and amateur treasure hunter. His son was a vet, while working in a Mexican cattle ranch had been told two stories about a lost gold mine. One in Arizona and the other California, with the story he had been given a Peralta map from a Mexican rancher, claiming to be a member of the Peralta family. He then gave the map along with both stories to his dad, who immediately took a keen interest. They decided to go to California first, they travelled across steep and rocky terrain. Adolph took a nasty fall and received a severe leg injury; it would affect him for the rest of his life and received a silver hip implant. After his retirement he decided to set his sights back to the stories of gold and go to the second location in Arizona.

He stopped by the Bark ranch, at the Western edge of the Superstitions before heading into the mountains. He met Tex Barkley the current owner, along with two prospectors and two farm hands. He freely talked about his map and adventure, which would take him to the famous treasure and wished to set right out and find it. His map contained a tall peak which Tex identified as Weaver's needle, he also helped him find the best camping ground. They found Willow springs to be most suited to a few weeks stay, as it is the closest source of water from Weaver's needle which was only two miles away.

Tex advised him it was not a good idea to go now, he should wait till the cooler months. If he could not wait, he would at least accompany him when he got back in a few days. The next again morning Ruth could not wait, he managed to convince the two farm hands to help guide him out to the campsite to start his expedition. They took him out to Willow Springs where he would make his camp, they stayed out with him to help set up before leaving. The two prospectors claimed to have come across Ruth in the days that followed, saying he was all right.

A week later nothing was heard from Ruth. Tex, having come back a week later was worried for Ruth's safety, he went out to check his campsite at willow springs. On arrival no one was there, his heavy boots were left at the camp, so he must have been wearing his light campsite shoes thinking he was close by. The authorities were contacted and after numerous searches nothing was found. Half a year later further searches conducted by the local newspaper found a skull in a bush by a canyon west of Weavers needle. The skull had two holes in the top, they were bullet holes, however no murder case was ever opened, being there were no suspects or motives to kill him.

It was recorded to be a natural death from exhaustion, wild animals were responsible for removing the head, dragging it from the body. Which was found by Tex, the next again day in west boulder canyon on top of a ridge, the skeleton was identified by the silver leg implant. His map was missing and among his affects was a piece of paper from his notebook. It stated the mine existed within a 5-mile diameter around Weaver's needle and about 2500 foot high up. He wrote 'veni vidi vici' and 'two hundred feet across from the cave' claiming to have found the mine prior to his death and possibly died from exhaustion while returning to his camp, disregarding the two bullet holes in his head.

James Cravey

1946 – 1948

James Cravey was a photographer who had just moved to Phoenix. He suffered severe injuries to his arm and leg, forcing him into retirement and in poor physical health. He was an amateur prospector and being in the area, was of course familiar with the dutchman story. One night in 1947 he had a dream of finding a lost mine in the mountains, which he was sure was the dutchman's. He took it as a sign he would be able to find it. Excited to go, he began to plan his expedition during the scorching summer months. He was not recommended to take the trip by friends, as his crippled arm and leg and now at 60 years old, would harden the trip which would already have been difficult.

He had experience prospecting but was not an expert of the Superstition area. It would not deter him from the urge to make the trip. He bought the supplies he would need, including a compass, navigation equipment, camping supplies, a pistol which would always be needed for snakes at the very least, he brought a long 50-foot rope, which he used in his dream to carry himself down into the mine pit.

From his disability, a friend later considered climbing down a rope would be out of his capability anyhow. With the final digging and prospecting tools, he was almost ready for the trip. He contacted Arizona helicopter services based in Phoenix, who helped find a pilot willing to take him out there and drop him along with his supplies off in the mountains. He said his goals were to find the mine which he claimed to know the location to and promised a share of the treasure for taking him there. Not convinced by treasure, they still allowed him to hire a helicopter for the trip.

They set off on in mid 1947. He brought eight days of provisions and five-gallon water tank. They attached the helicopter to the top of a trailer and drove out to the closest site they could take off from, which was four miles from Lebarge canyon. He was flown out and dropped off by the pilot who made the return journey. The idea of the trip would have Cravey make his trip and walk back out to town himself.

Once a few days has passed when he was due back, he failed to report he had come back to town. His disappearance was reported to sheriff by the helicopter services and missing persons case was opened. They could not use a helicopter to begin the search, as poor weather conditions along with the cost would not permit. They could not air lift dogs to help search when the weather had cleared, as bringing dogs into a confined space was not recommended.

The weather cleared over the next couple of days, they finally managed to do arial search. No sign of him was found on the first fly over. Days later a search landed at the campsite he was dropped off at. The site was found abandoned, with all the food and water intact if not all there. There was no more than two days' worth of ash in the firepit as well. Several affects were missing, taken by Cravey at the time he last left camp. These included mining tools, backpack, rope, canteen, and his pistol.

Looking like he is going to excavate soon after the arrival of his trip.

There were no clear footprints to suggest the direction he had travelled. The next again day a search party with dogs looked across Lebarge canyon for any signs of his whereabouts. They looked down a slope and found his bedding, food and canteen which was almost full before the dogs lost the scent. The search ended after two weeks; it was not until February the next again year before hikers in the area had come across bones. They found a skeleton with the skull missing, South of Weavers needle. It contained a wallet identifying the remains belonged to Cravey. With a further search his skull was found in a canyon East of Weavers needle. It was determined a natural death, from a combination of his poor health and being exposed in rough conditions during the worst of the summer months.

Abandoned camp site
1958

Through the summer, the Pinal County sheriff was contacted by hikers, requesting a unit to respond. The sheriff arrived at the North of the mountains finding two young students shook up. They had clearly seen something to disturb them so much. This was common, with the history of the mountains and ghost stories, young people would occasionally come up and get scared.

The sheriff had the hikers point him in the direction he was to travel, which was a bit further up in the mountain.

He left the students and continued on by himself. He soon came across an abandoned campsite. There were heavy scuff marks around the ground, indicating there could have been a violent confrontation, food was also scattered over the campfire area. Items left around the place included a Geiger counter and a gun cleaning kit, though no weapon was present. The sheriff was horrified to find a sleeping bag spread out over a nearby bush, stained in blood. He quickly realized he needed to call in the situation, something terrible had happened. With a further search there were clothes and letters found, all name labels from the manufacturer which could help identify where they came from were ripped out, the address had been removed from the letters. Nothing further ever came of it.

Jesse Capen
2009

A huge believer in the mine legend, would set out nine hundred miles from his home, travelling all the way to the Superstitions to search for the gold. His trip was to last two weeks, by day four of the trip, a vehicle was found abandoned in an unauthorised parking area. Nearby to the car is an abandoned campsite, which contained Jesse's driver's license, money as well as camping supplies.

Within months after his disappearance, three other treasure hunters vanished. Adding to a total of over twenty treasure hunters, who had now died in search for the mine. Later another treasure hunter came across three skeletons, they belonged to the later missing men, who had all died of exposure. Two years after Jesse had vanished, a logbook left on top of tortilla mountain was found containing Jesse's initials, confirming he had made it to the top at some point of the trip.

The body was found three years after he disappeared, lodged in a crevasse which was not accessible from above, just half a mile from the campsite. Questioning just how it got there, he might have got lost and climbed up high to find directions or have been looking out from a high point, close by his campsite, where he fell from a ledge to his death.

After all the stories surrounding the Dutchman legend there must be some tangible evidence for it to exist. There is physical evidence to show building works have been constructed in the mountains, found in Lebarge canyon. The Superstitions do not hold many trees mostly bushes, but some trees are found in canyons, one of which being Lebarge. A considerable amount of tree stumps has been found cut from long ago, along with evidence of an old camp site around the area. It was initially expected to be an army construction, as they had forts and a trail going by the mountains. Officials were adamant they never had cut down trees or made any construction in the mountains. They did not spend long enough in the open wilderness to have needed a construction; they were unaware of why so many trees may have all been cut.

From Waltz's description of his mine to Reinhardt, he said inside the tunnel, leading up to the entrance of the pit there is wooden shelfs, columns and supports inside the structures. It is believed the timber taken from Lebarge canyon, was the source of all the cut timber in the mine. From the canyon the stumps could have been hauled away in either direction, going further into Lebarge or the other way to tortilla mountain. Which coincidently has a spring at its base, just as Waltz describes having a water source nearby his mine. It could be that Weavers needle, being the more popular peak in the area, has been continually misidentified with Tortilla Mountain over the many stories. Which solidified Weavers needle at the centre of the mystery, misdirecting the search away from the mine which could beyond Tortilla Mountain.

Evidence of documentation gives credence to the story is hard to come by, but some does exist which proves existence of gold. It does not prove the existence of the fabled mine, at the very least it does show that gold has come from out of the mountain. It may have been transported back from a mine further away, being taken through Superstitions, when the Apache raided the miners. They had more use for the burrows than gold, so took them and left the gold where it lay. It was later found by the various individuals who came by gold in the mountain. Gold just being left in the mountains would not consider the multiple specific references to the mine described by Waltz, the Peralta's, the two soldiers, Joe Dearing and the boy working at Novinger's ranch, being an actual mine.

It would not make sense to buy and carry mining equipment, just to head out there and pick it up from the ground, there is enough stories to suggest there is a mine in the mountains. There are shipping orders from Wells Fargo, proving that Waltz had shipped $240 thousand dollars' worth of high-grade ore to be smelted. He was getting it from somewhere, the idea he was just stealing ore from the Vulture mine he was working during his time in Arizona is unlikely. He would have to get away with taking so much undetected. Then to lie in his old age, all the way to his death bed, lying to those he grew close with and trusted, would serve no purpose in the end. There are considerations that over the years, the Apache would adorn their sacred mountains with gifts to appease the thunder god. They could have left golden artifacts at shrines, during Jacob's time prospecting he could have stumbled into a cave or sacred place and looted it, being the source of his gold. The idea stands out as not fitting with the history of the mine, going back further than just Waltz to the natives who had precious metal pointing the mountain out as its source. It would not fit Doctor Thorne receiving gold ore, not golden artifacts and the Apache. Natives would have had to source the gold from somewhere, even at Rich hill where it is so availably to pick up, they could have found gold and left it in caves at tribute.

One of the natives who befriended American's told of a cave that contained many valuables. He was travelling through the Superstitions when he came across it himself. It was the site of a battle between the Apache and soldiers. The soldiers had been caught out and retreated to hold out in the cave. It was not enough to hold out against the Apache who had more men and they stormed the cave killing all the soldiers. They had a lot of valuable possessions on them, the Apache did not touch any possessions over their spiritual beliefs and left them intact where they lay in the cave. When the Indian told the Americans they decided they should check it out and take what they could find. They were led to a cave in the mountains but found nothing. Either the native had changed his mind and took them to a different area for fear of retaliation for leading white men to treasure or it had been previously found and looted.

There exists a famous golden matchbox, made from the gold ore coming from Jacob Waltz himself. It stays in the ownership of a private collector and rarely makes exhibits to the public, nevertheless it still exists. Being assessed for its gold signature, the atomic make up of gold is unique to other known gold sources all over the world, which provides a comparison to estimate its geographical source. The golden matchbox was not identified to any mine source, meaning it could have come from the elusive lost mine.

From the many trails used by hikers and treasure hunters, the mountains are regularly explored. One unusual discovery found hundreds of pairs of light Mexican sandals bundled together in a crevasse at the side of a canyon wall. It is believed the sandals belonged to Peralta mining expeditions, they would leave them behind as the terrain got rough and would collect them on the way back. On this occasion they never did, either it coincided with a massacre, or they chose to leave them behind leaving the mountains a different route. Showing evidence to large movements of people through the area decades before.

There a Plateau with deeply eroded trail leading up to it. Left behind as evidence from a Spanish trail, as they were bringing livestock up there to hold and protect them during their mining expeditions. Hundreds of animals were used to transporting gold back. In the years the Peralta family work at their mine, they needed a temporary area to hold their animals. The only trail up to a large plateau was eventually worn deep from a prolonged use, leading hundreds of animals up to the top. Surrounding the plateau is thick vegetation, which would keep animals herded together and prevent them escaping. They were kept up there until the mine workings were finished, then taken down to transport the ore. The site also served as a look out over to the mine, only a few men with rifles were needed to protect all the animals and miners. This hillside has been found and photographed, with a single heavily eroded trail up it. The location of the mine from the plateau is not clear. From Dutch hunters making their own travels and discoveries of clues related to the trail, the exact locations are usually kept to themselves which disorganises a coherent search.

From the legends surrounding the Superstitions, stories attract many to search. Treasure hunters and writers have claimed to have found it, publishing their 'proof' in an all telling book or sold the story to the media receiving publicity. Anyone claiming to have found the mine cannot be taken seriously and burdens the rest of their story with doubt. Surely finding the mine, with its wealth beyond imagining would never be best suited in a book, the location kept hidden only to the author with nothing but their story as proof. Finding the site would be of incredible historical value and would gain huge attention. Its importance would keep it from commercial mining but to exist as a wonder. Claiming to have found it and keeping it to themselves makes no sense, mining it would be illegal so you could not gain financially. Mining illegally would require a long running discrete commercial operation. There would also not receive the recognition of being the one to have found the place which is what they are setting out to do.

It is possible mining may still exist illegally in the area. Several tunnels and pits have been found and photographed all over the area, but none have ever proved without a doubt to be the Dutchman's. Illegal mining would surely be no doubt lucrative, therefore protected and leading to the high number of murders for anyone venturing too close. One Dutch hunter, walking over a peak came across an almost invisible trail, it was so old it had been almost overgrown. He followed it down over the ridge, leading to three large boulders. Just round the trail from there, he almost stepped on a camouflage net, which was hiding a large hole. It had wooden ladders leading down, climbing down it was too dark to see and so climbed back out. After making it out, the sound of voices from three distinctive men, sounded up through the valley. Looking down the men were moving directly towards him, carrying with them heavy automatic weapons. With only a pistol he had to quickly leave the area. The encounter was very suspicious of illegal mining which could explain deaths involving bullet wounds to the head.

Likely, between the earthquake in 1887 earthquake and the floods in 1891. The resulting damage may have destroyed any trace of the mine. In the times the stories take place, the Apache were a huge threat guarding the mountains, hardly anyone would venture out there without real purpose. Of those few who did go, we were left with multiple stories from all of those with connection to the gold. Some gained the knowledge of its location, others stumbled across it, even those looking for it were able to find it. It may have been difficult but was possible.

Waltz claimed to have covered it over at the end of his last trip. Indian stories tell of an old mine which continually attracted white men over time. To deter more destruction of their sacred land a group was tasked to spend a full winter up there. They were to completely covering up the mine and return the land to its natural state, removing all traces of human habitation. This would leave the area even more difficult to find, even in its proximity where it is buried would be difficult to spot. Since it was so easily found numerous times, now attracting hundreds of people to explore every year, specially looking for the mine and it can no longer be found, was covered over if not destroyed. The entrance would require being dug out to uncover it. Digging has been made illegal to deter further destruction to the land. If the mine was to be searched for the right reasons, aside from adventurous a group including local experts, all well-equipped may someday have the chance to uncover and preserve the mine for its historic importance.

The reality is many hunters travelling up there are inexperienced. They are compelled to travel over the roughest terrain during the toughest of months, risking death from exposure. Danger could be circumvented by reducing the secrecy of hunting for gold. Information related to searches would need to be shared publicly. Using modern technology, trips would be much safer done at the appropriate time of year. To penetrate the ground surface without digging, radar can now be used. Compiling information to the mine and mapping out all clues, to find the location within the famous 5-mile radius Northeast of Weavers needle and Tortilla Mountain. With help modern drones to help scout and picture areas quickly, could lead to the narrow canyon described and eventually find the location within there.

El Dorado

The mythical city of limitless treasure, holding the richest archaeological relics of the New World kept in the golden Meso America city, lost in deep uncharted jungles of the Amazon. The real story behind its conception, has created the most famous fantasy city in the world. Its endless search, told by Amazonians led to their torture, death, and subjugation, brought to them for keeping their greatest prize a secret.

1300-1400

Portugal was making a rise in power; they dominated the seas with its navy using it to colonise islands in the Atlantic. They established trade routes down to African kingdoms, across the Indian ocean and into Asia. A better route from carrying everything over land, being more labour intensive and open to bandit attacks. Ancient Greeks understood the earth was round, during this medieval age scholars believed the earth was considerably smaller than what we know it to be today.

The New World

1492

This led Christopher Columbus, a Genoese man who became a sailor for Portugal. To hypothesize, if they sail west, they will make it straight to Asia by going round the Atlantic. They purpose would be to make an even shorter route and open themselves directly to a huge market. A newly discovered route would make himself rich. Portugal's government was not convinced of this small earth theory, Spain was looking to compete with Portugal's rising influence and seen the potential for a new trade route being worth funding a ship to make the journey. They commissioned funding three ships to navigate west. The entire journey took three months, stopping off once at Grand Canaria to resupply with food and fresh water. They set off west for a further five weeks before making landfall. They believed themselves to be in Japan, unaware they had set foot onto an entirely new land which is now the island of Hispaniola, off the coast of South America.

First meeting and trading with the island's natives, Spanish sailors noticed the glistening of golden jewellery in their possession. Immediately attracting the new arrivals attention, interested in finding the source of the metal. On Hispaniola, thirty-nine men were left to begin colonisation, creating a settlement in Columbus's absence. He would return to inform the court of the discovery of a new continent, containing new exotic foods and people, with a bountiful supply of natural resources, the people there living comfortably on such a rich place. He took back with him artifacts from the New

World including captures natives, tobacco, and stuffed tropical animals.

When he returned, he rose to be an instant celebrity, having ventured into the unknown and coming back to tell such a wonderous tale. The next again year, Spain commissioned a further seventeen ships to sail out and claim these lands for Spain. When he returned to Hispaniola, the thirty-nine settlers were all found dead. Killed by natives under the rule of the chief who took insult at the new arrivals. In the land of this newly discovered people, there were gold mines which the Spanish had taken over, angering the chief. Native Americans were rounded up and executed publicly by the settlers for this, further dividing settlers and natives.

They again took control of the mine for themselves and began to extract ore. It was not a big mine, when it soon ran out Columbus exaggerated the volume of gold found and took five hundred slaves to subsidise profits, even suggesting they should open a slave trade. He noted in letters back to Spain, how easily the natives could be conquered and all enslaved. The large-scale enslavement Columbus took, having the locals rounded up and imprisoned was the breaking point for tribes and they fought back. Spanish having superior weapons, beat them to submission and made them pay gold in tribute. Forcing gold to be retrieved from their lands, either imprisoning or cutting the hands off those who did not offer enough. Terrified, many left fleeing to remote parts of the island, they were chased by Spaniards on horseback with their hunting dogs. Columbus returned to

Spain, to defend his actions starting a conflict. With satisfaction from the throne, he was allowed to return to Hispaniola. A member of government was sent along to assess the situation unfolding in the new world. Soon after they arrived, Columbus was arrested once his crimes were immediately exposed towards the natives, as well as to the Spanish, he was imprisoned and immediately sent back to Spain.

Though it is still celebrated to this day, the arrival of Europeans in the Americas was the first contact. It is now realized he was not the first to traverse the Atlantic and find the Americas. Voyages from Vikings had previously reached Nova Scotia, they did not build a permanent residence. The voyages Columbus led were able to sustain prolonged habitation. In doing so, he left behind his name as being its finder. Conveniently ignoring his real legacy, destroying the natives, and opening the Americas to up colonisation. The decimation and enslavement of a population which he considered an inferior, just another resource to be exploited due to their inferior technology to be able to defend themselves, pitting spears against cannon fire. As a result, most of native American history, knowledge, culture, and contribution to the world was lost.

Aztec Empire

1519

After the arrival of Europeans, word of its riches travelled fast. Further expeditions were formed for conquest by making alliances and with military dominance by the Spanish conquistadors. They attracted individuals specifically out there for domination of the lands, taking native wealth by force and returning home, heroes with fortunes. The time before arrival was at the height of the Aztec empire, much of Mexico was under rule of its capital Tenochtitlan, its emperor Moctezuma being paid tribute with taxes coming all over the empire, which was built from the submission of smaller tribes following military expansion. Much of the surrounding tribes despised their rule, others were still at war for their independence. Meanwhile Spanish was setting off from Cuba for their new conquest, led by Hernan Cortez with five hundred and thirty Europeans, along with their horses and dogs.

The natives were shocked coming across these new arrivals. A ship was first noticed anchored off the coast. There was no word to describe such large objects floating, some lake side societies had built small rafts, made from woven reeds or dugout canoes but nothing comparable the size of a ship worthy of sailing the sea. They could only describe what they were seeing, as men riding on the backs of floating islands.

They were amazed with the presentation of the Spanish, wearing in comparison to themselves fine and unique clothing, full of colour. Their possessions were far beyond their own capabilities, they revered the new settlers as Sun gods. The light would shine off their armour, also controlling such large horses made them look far beyond themselves, particularly that of Cortez. After initial conflicts, the natives though far superior in number, were terrified by the sound of the invaders cannon fire, it exploded like nothing they had ever experienced the sound shaking through them, erupting the earth beneath their feet as projectiles crashed into the earth. The chaos caused from the sound of gun fire and the sight of men riding horses was terrifying. The natives had never encountered such animals, they believed the men to be attached to the horses, being a centaur like creature. They halted immediately in their charge which would have overwhelmed Cortez and pushed them all back to the sea, they instead considering diplomacy.

Some tribes were quick to side with Spanish, with on-going tribal warfare, smaller native groups were threatened into submission and despised paying tribute for Aztec rule. They told they only had small amounts of gold compared to the capital, which resided further up the coast inland, there they would find the material they were most interested in.

Word of a new pale people coming from the West Coast, had just reached the capital. The empire already contained a diverse mix of people, from all over America. The arrival of Europeans was not of much concern as being a threat. When Cortez docked further up the Coast, they were met by emissaries giving them golden gifts and exchanged knowledge of where they were each from, including the information that the Aztec king possessed a lot of gold, which is what they wanted to hear the most, thinking they just wanted to visit to see it for themselves.

How much gold they had was thought comparable to the large number of golden gifts received from the representatives of the emperor. This was seen comparatively thought by the Europeans, to be just a tiny portion to a far greater reserve they were keeping for themselves. Family members were advising Moctezuma not to trust the Spanish, they were known to be raiders and Cortez was currently negotiating with those not in favour of Aztec rule to overthrow them. It was a huge mistake to have sides with Cortez as it turns out, it only took a few hundred Spanish to overthrow and destroy the entire empire.

They travelled through the jungle battling native tribes that lived along the way, they were all part of the Aztec empire. Continually taking small loses added up for the conquistadors, they could not sustain many casualties with their already small number. As they travelled and met more people not in favour with the Aztecs, they joined and added to their ranks of native warriors. Many were convinced to join rather than fight and made up ninety five percent of Cortez army. Fighting for their freedom taken away by the Aztecs, convinced usurping them was in their best interests. They negotiated with every tribe on their route before reaching the heart of the empire. They would subject natives to the laws of Spain, making accusations of treason and massacring entire towns who would not join them.

Arriving at the capital, the city resided on floating pontoons made from woven reeds. They floated in the middle of lake Texcoco. Access to the great city was made through a giant causeway built with wooden logs which were hammered into the lake with a walkway built on top. They entered to the city and were welcomed, being allowed to stay. Once again, the Spanish denounce all traces of reason, after being shown a kindness from their hosts, immediately became paranoid and plotted against Moctezuma. They kidnapped him during a meeting in a temple, they brought more guards than the emperor had and surrounded him, taking him back to their residence where he was imprisoned in his own city. They would use him as a puppet to take over the empire.

The people were outraged which rose fears for a revolt. The Spanish fear was used to justify further crimes kidnapping and torturing citizens for information. They had previously used tactics against the natives of ambushing and slaughtering them by the thousands, during ceremonial holidays to a huge success. When festivities were going on they were unarmed civilians. They used this strategy to devastating effect deciding to unleash the same horror in Tenochtitlan. They surrounded a festival centre blocking off its exits and attacked the unarmed Aztec noblemen. They left only the few alive to puppet the remains of the empire.

A huge ransom was to be collected for Moctezuma; it was so great a cost it would have taken months to bring in so much gold from all over the empire. Only a fraction of the wealth ever reached the Spanish before they killed Moctezuma. The people eventually turned against their captured emperor. The rest of the gold was said to have been taken back from its routes travelling to pay the ransom, instead taken directed to a city called Petite where it was hidden.

Sieged inside the city, the natives removed sections of the causeways entering the city, preventing the retreat of the Spanish back to their ships, and were surrounded. They crafted temporary bridges, which would be used under the cover of darkness to quickly sneak over, carrying as much gold as they could take with them. The bridge was spotted after only half the army had crossed and were surrounded by Aztecs coming over by canoes. They climbed onto their bridge and destroyed it, plunging dozens of Spanish soldiers in the lake, including Cortez himself who had to be dragged out to safety. Most of the gold was spilt and lost in the waters, with treasures and dead Spanish filling in the damaged bridge, it again allowed further crossing to be made, over the backs of their dead countrymen.

1521

They managed to retreat and regroup, not receiving many troubles from natives with smallpox spreading. They made camp for a few months at a settlement, where they were able to train their remaining army for the final attack. With the rapid decline of the empire from disease and war, Tenochtitlan was finally weak enough to be sieged once more time, for the final battle. They attacked from both land and boat and the city finally fell. After victory they tore down traditional architecture and temples, building their own structures over the foundations. As occupation went on word of further riches came, telling of a lost city of gold.

The true end of the native people came from their own hatred, by competing tribes who made up their own empire. This allowed for the civil war between Meso Americans to begin, propagated by the few Spanish who promised their own freedoms and leading them to the entire collapse the society, those not dying in war were killed soon after from disease. Though paying an annual tribute towards the empire may have been an inconvenience, it served to band them together as one people with the potential to stand together and fight off a more powerful invader such as the Spanish. With their own turmoil and desire for freedom, they led themselves directly to the loss of an entire continent.

Incan Empire

1532

The Incas originally descended from migratory Asia tribes. They crossed over from East Asia. Across a land bridge made from ice, connecting Asia to America from 22000 BC until the end of the last ice age. At some point they made it to inhabit high in the Peruvian region of the Andes at least 16000BC. As thousands of years passed. The people moved high in the Andes where 2500BC the beginnings of Inca people started around Lake Titicaca.

The lake provided fish and reeds used to make floating structures, a foundation to build on top of. As well as supplying material to make most everyday household items. They farmed the few crops able to be grown as such high altitudes and mined metals from surrounding mountains. Populations existed all-round the lake and to the southern shores Tiwinaku, it features huge construction of stonework, making an impressive city but not being from Incan culture but from other people before their time who lived nearby.

They existed alongside the Inca until their collapse around 1000AD, leaving the Incas to be the largest collective in the Andes ever since. They extended their influence over to warmer and more fertile locations. Where they built the new capital, Cusco in 1100AD. Over the next four hundred years before colonialism, they flourished and expanded all over the Western South American mountains, conquering and assimilating many other smaller tribes around them. They are credited for making huge constructions and lived in relative peace.

One of those looking to seek their personal fortune and glory in a following expedition was Francisco Pizarro. Arriving to the Americas being lured from its tales. They docked to the East of the mainland, crossed the narrowest landmass, and rebuilt their ships at the other side of the ocean to sail down to Peru. There had received word of a new empire existing other than the Aztecs, which was far bigger and richer. They travelled in search of the Incas, which were thought to have a population of up to twenty million.

Following a month of slow jungle trekking they eventually stumbled to the edges of the Incan empire, where they found small villages and met the inhabitants. They were pointed to roads leading to larger settlements, with incredible architecture of temples and buildings the higher they climbed. More than anything else, alongside incredible cultural achievements they seen what they cared for most, gold. The heart of the empire existed in high territory up in the Andes. Where they were to reach the capital Cusco. They climbed higher each day coming into more frequent contact with undiscovered peoples. Natives were amazed by the war horses accompanying the party. They were thought of as half human half deer like creatures. On their travels to the capital, they traded as they went to make their supplies last as long as they could.

The strange army were noticed by on the way up and word had made it to the capital. An army was banded to set out to find the one hundred and sixty-eight soldiers. They decided to meet them and find out who these travellers are and what they had come for. Initially they were considered to be friendly by the Incas, they were quick to put down any hopes of their reasonability, attacking the native's superior army from a distance with their superior crossbows and cannon fire. Killing up to five thousand of the Incans. They possessed armour and steel weapons along with gunpowder, making them difficult to kill against a people with little to protect them. Among the battle the Incan emperor was captured and imprisoned to be ransomed for gold and art.

Over the following year they stayed alongside their prisoner as eleven tonnes of precious metal was gathered from across the empire, to pay the ridiculous demands set to make the men rich beyond imagining for their return to Spain. As part of a traditional Spanish custom, they never considered to have enough gold for satisfy their greed. They kept desiring more, they reasoned if they could produce so much in a year, then there is always bound to be more, in some unlimited supply. They proceeded to sack Cusco, taking it for all its wealth, going as far to taking their bowls, plates, and jars after they had finished pulling apart their temples.

They never did release the Incan king, they feared an army would be raised during the slow descent down from the Andes, carrying half the looted city with them. So, in accordance with Spanish tradition, killed the king and enslaved the population. Their buildings were knocked down and built over with Spanish construction, which were nowhere near as advanced as Incan stone work using huge interlocked dry stones, all perfectly positioned to allow them the flexibility to preserve them for thousands of years.

1536

After years of occupancy, legends begin reaching the conquistadors of a new city. It sat by a lake, made from crystal and gold. It was ruled by a king they called El Rey Dorado, 'the golden king.' He would cover himself in gold powder stuck to his body using sap during a ritual. It marked the passing rule from the previous king to his nephew, named the Zepa to crown the next great leader. The ceremony was indeed real, it took place around lake Guatavita. A raft would be constructed and decorated in colourful art and emeralds. The new ruler indeed covered in gold dust, adorning him with spiritual power from its connectivity to God from its colour and corrosive properties. There God is named Chiminiguagua, he is attributed to creating the earth, sun, and moon. Taking the raft into the middle of the lake, gold offerings would be dropped into its waters. The Zepa would enter the water, washing the gold powder off. Spectators round the lake would throw in around fifty percent of their golden objects as further tribute, granting good blessings for the future.

1537

Through all odds one expedition, setting out the next again year led by Hermenes de Casida, along with nine hundred soldiers. They were looking to find a land route to Peru, to save deconstructing ships. They travelled deep into unexplored jungle through central Colombia. They detoured from their journey after hearing the rumours of this rich golden city. They were the Muisca, they do not exist as a single collection of people but was an alliance between three regions, each possessing its own king. The grandest king being the overall spiritual authority, to speak on behalf of all people. They were an advanced tribe with incredible gold working skills, making intricate jewellery and trinkets. They often mixed an alloy of gold, silver, and copper to make their jewellery and crafted from platinum, which they were close enough to the incredibly rare deposit. They did not have immediate access to much gold themselves but through vast trade networks they had built across South America brought in gold, becoming a centre for its crafting. The Spanish could not resist getting there and taking over this wonderous place, stealing all the gold they could lay their hands on, destroying it to ruin.

The Música, like all other natives, did not have a single currency. It was certainly not attributed directly to the value of gold representing wealth, rather a commodity used for trade along with everything else. They valued rare coco beans closer to a centralised currency rather than metal. They used gold as a decorative material, with spiritual links being the same colour as the sun, giving it considerable religious importance but was not to be excessively collected and stored in quantity, not valued more than any other traded goods.

From their different understanding of gold, they did not realize the effect it had on the men, who used it as the single most valuable intermediary between all trade. They did not understand it existed to serve a decorative purpose beyond their own appreciation, giving the status of wealth and power. Overwhelmed with the amount of wealth being flaunted, they assumed the native's jewellery only could have only been a fraction on display, much more must be stored away. By their logic, a person of wealth would only have so much of their money in their jewellery and fine clothes. So, the same must have been true for the Muisca.

After their golden possessions were exhausted. They turned to the lake to provide the next source of gold. Lazaro Fonte and Hernan de Quesada made a manual effort to drain the lake by hand bailing it out with buckets. Only being able to lower the water level by ten feet, they recovered around one hundred thousand dollars' worth, but was not what they had believed it should have contained there had to be deeper. The imagination of what else they have secretly hidden away spread out of control creating in the minds of the Spanish, El Dorado the golden city. No longer the ritual involving a golden man, but they must have so much gold, buildings would be finished or made with it, where they would finally find gold beyond measure. The reality was not having much economic use for gold and would offer it freely as tribute. Managing to make it to the Muisca king, after hearing he was rumoured to have so much of it, even the fabled lake Guatavita filled with hundreds of years' worth of offerings, they did not come across as much as expected and were disappointed having taken everything from them it was not enough.

The Muisca were expert craftsmen of gold, trading it into their lands. They had their own natural resources of emeralds, copper, and salt. Salt was of extremely important as it would be compacted into blocks called salt cakes, they would be broken apart when needed and rubbed into meats. This was not to season it but added in large quantities preserved meats for storage, during journeys through South America. The gold the Muisca did possess would still have been considerable before being taken as they worked using it so often. The real wealth they had across all other resources was not of interest to the Spanish.

After early contact with the Muisca, they would regularly come across platinum workings along other precious metals. Platinum is a soft metal, easy for working also sharing non corrodible properties along with gold. When found the Spanish it dismissed, though to be unripe silver, unaware of its true rarity surpassing gold itself, they left it as scrap. Gold coin counterfeits were even being made from platinum, it became such a problem for Spain's gold economy, they took the nations platinum reserves and dumped it in the ocean, in a despite attempt to prevent gold becoming unstable. It goes to show Spain's lust for gold was an insatiable hunger, completely overlooking the Americas actual worth kept in culture, arts, architecture and full of other resources, all dismissed for what they already knew back home.

In northern parts of Colombia there lived another society, advanced in farming and gold working like the Muisca. They are called the Tairona, living in the Colombian mountains, they built road networks from stone. Allowing trade, as well as serving as an alarm to carry sounds of footsteps, alerting them to presence of travellers. There skills in battle were exceptional, they prevented colonisation, holding off far better than many larger empires, remaining in conflict for over 75 years. They gained much respect from their ferocity, like the

Muisca they had plenty gold but did not value it past religious interests.

Over time around lake Guatavita, they began receiving more stories of vast quantities of gold further North. They left the Muisca to start chasing the seven golden cities of Cibola, travelling all through Mexico, making it as far as Arizona. They never found enough to ever satisfy their need after all their travels. As time went on, they would periodically hear rumours of numerous golden cities existing just close enough to reach. Each time reigniting excitement for their discovery, they would rush off as fast as they could and usually fail, taking huge casualties to their expeditions. Natives were all too happy to keep telling tales of gold, just over the next valley to move their occupiers on.

1541

Stories reignited the drive to venture deeper into the Amazon basin, setting off from Colombia looking for treasure sent several parties searching only to fail. Traversing dense jungle, a number of unfortunate fates from creatures, clashes with natives, and being in an unfamiliar place ending up lost facing starvation and dehydration are never far away. Over spilling with vegetation, hiding amongst the thick plant cover are poisonous giant centipede's, disease carrying mosquito's, venomous spiders, snakes, frogs, nests of bullet ants whose single bite is so excruciating it compared to a gunshot. Not to mention the larger animals' jaguars, caiman, and piranhas, making expeditions increasingly more dangerous than navigation alone.

During one of these failed explorations, led by Gonzalo Pizarro a relative of Francisco Pizarro, the conquer of Inca's, also accompanying was Francisco Oriana. Blazing trails with machetes, they set out to find a hidden valley rich in gold and cinnamon. At the beginning of the trip, they set out with three hundred and forty Spaniards, along with a few thousand natives. They came across huge difficulties, suffering from disease and running low on food supplies. They resorted to killing and eating their Indian guides, who helped them to communicate and find routes to travel. After Gonzales fell further ill, he could no longer keep traveling. They split the party up, sending Oriana down to the Amazon River. Which was meant to be a short trip to find food and come back to the rest of the group. They came across animals to hunt but the trail too steep to make it back. Though Oriana's trip never returned to bring food to a sick Gonzales, he had managed to recover enough to make it out himself.

Oriana reported the first ever expedition along the Amazon River, seeing many flourishing cities across its banks, supporting millions of people the length of the huge basin. All filled with arts, they even had come across a group of female Amazonian warriors. When returned to Spain he told his account, he was accredited to be the first man to travel the Amazon, bringing back with him its wonderous tales.

He later returned to travel it again, getting his group lost in one of the many tributaries. Himself and his loyalist sailors were abandoned and left on an island following a mutiny. The river was not travelled for over a hundred years following the Spanish expeditions. On return to the Amazon these huge cities were not seen and so thought Oriana had made it all up, following the destruction the conquest had left behind, these large cities would have fallen apart, left abandoned to be quickly consumed from the rapidly growing rainforest.

1580

The next effort to drain the lake of Guatavita, cut a huge notch in the hillside surrounding the lake. This time it was drained by twenty meters. Revealing a further four hundred thousand dollars' worth of gold. Efforts were made to dig the notch deeper and draining more away, the hillside collapsed killing a number of the workers caught amongst falling rock. This huge effort to cut out an entire hillside a second time was too costly for the gold recovered, to make it a viable endeavour.

1595

The last European explorer to make a search for the fabled city of El Dorado was a British man, Walter Raleigh a personal friend to the Queen of England. Through his political connections managed to get funding to make a trip across the Atlantic to the Americas. After arrival he heard of the lake filled with gold. It was meant to be located far inland never being found. He made up the location and name of the lake, he called Parime and set out to find it. While searching like the Spanish before, there was huge difficulty with supplies running low and being slowed down from thick vegetation and disease. The expedition failed and he was imprisoned for 12 years, after he was allowed to go back to search. With the accordance he does not interfere with Spanish territory, which would lead to an international incident. At the beginning of the second expedition, he immediately entered Spanish territory trying to take their outpost, the ensuing fight between the two groups broke out and the British had to retreat. Walter was sent back to England to be executed for breaking the only agreement of his exploration.

The centuries that followed never did reveal any such golden city. With the native population being destroyed, no further reports were coming in to move conquest away with the promising the golden city. It became widely accepted El Dorado was never a real city, just an exaggeration. Through their own greed for gold, constant efforts to take more led to the creation of a city full of it. Once it had been idealised, no amount of gold ever found would have ever compared and satisfied the vision of what they had created.

So compelled for the search, they went as far to torture and kill for its location. Which would never have been found. They failed to value any other aspect of the cultures they came across for what they were. Finally finding a place which used rituals involving gold freely given to a lake and actually being able to find the source of the legend itself, was not good enough.

1898

As time went on El Dorado was realized to have been a myth, its source at Lake Guatavita was not forgotten. The next attempt to recover gold from the real Eldorado, came from British adventurers. They attempted to drain the lake by pumping the water out. They managed to remove the water but when the lake drained down to four feet, the bed contained a thick mud. Extracting gold was difficult and only recovered six hundred dollars' worth with forty objects. It was a commercial failure. Furthermore, making the attempt a disaster, soon after the lake was drained the thick mud dried and hardened encasing any gold that remained making it impossible to retrieve and went bankrupt.

1909

The last commercial attempt was made by an English company. They dug a tunnel underneath the lake to drain it, the soft mud inside the tunnel could not support the weight of earth above and collapsed the dry lake naturally filled up days after. After 1965, excavations to the lake were banned and the site left to be protected. Far too late to preserve any of the culture that had been long destroyed centuries before.

One reason draining lake Guatavita was not as fruitful as anticipated, could be through the ongoing removal of golden offerings to the lake. Thievery is not by any means a modern invention, even individuals from the Incan empire following the celebrations could have gone by the lakeside to loot artifacts. Though they are not as valuable to the natives as the Spanish, they still have trade potential and natives did not live all equally, they had those in power with more and those working who had less. The longevity of the Muisca and particularly this tradition of a golden king, is not clear. Thousands of years' worth of kings and offerings could create this lake filled with gold, compared to a few hundred years of this ritual happening several times, only when crowning a new king once every 20 years.

1969

A golden raft was discovered inside of a cave. It was found wrapped with fabric stored in a ceramic pot, near the village Lazaro Fonte. The raft depicting multiple golden figures riding on it, it shows important people escorting the Muisca chief covered in gold. Bringing their offerings out to the lake, part of the El Dorado ceremony. The piece was created using a wax casting, smelting a mix of mostly gold with silver and copper it was poured inside the cast, creating the figure any time between 600AD until the arrival of Spanish. A further search of the cave revealed nothing else, so seemingly hidden after Spanish arrival by someone keeping it from them. Whoever had left it were unable to return to claim it, probably from contracting small pox. It could have been an offering left inside a sacred site since it is the only offering its more likely a hidden item.

At the height of colonialism, Spain took all the gold they could find and shipped it all back home. They brought so much from all over the Americas, their own economy collapsed. It was largely based around the supply of gold which was being flooded into Spain. Many ships loaded with treasure did not make the journey and sank carrying all its cargo to the bottom of the ocean, still it did not make any difference they had so much coming in the value plummeted.

Overall, the South American's were destroyed and looted, taking far more away than just the value of gold, which was all melted from its expert craftmanship into coins. The heritage of the people and their cultural knowledge lost with their destruction. The Spanish did not benefit past the few individuals returning home incredibly rich, in the long term they had also thrown away a lot of platinum. With their economy collapsing there was no pay off for either side, the world lost out on so much from the greed on a few.

There was never any large-scale invasion from the Eastern world. It did not take tens of thousands of well trained and provisioned troops, sweeping across these new civilisations of Aztecs and Incas and those smaller and in between, with their huge advantages of weaponry to topple an entire continent. Only a few hundred or couple of thousand, managing to convince their own people turning against themselves was in their own interest. Not that much convincing was needed, they were not always on good terms with each other, they thought they wanted to avoid being assimilated with part of larger empire. Deciding to align with Europeans as a rally point for rebellion, together turning it to ruin.

Wonders of the Ancient World

225BC

Several Byzantian writers and poets, after travelling throughout the Mediterranean recorded noteworthy experiences. Regularly featured in these lists are seven sites which became known as wonders of the ancient world. A collection of greatest achievements from the heights of great past civilizations, drawing travellers from across the world to see these spectacles for themselves. Across the world at the same time, there were many other ancient structures, these were not as well known to the Byzantines frequenting across the Mediterranean and Aegean. The only structure left standing happens to be considerably older than the rest, the Great Pyramid of Giza. The rest have been lost over the centuries, only their descriptions left behind, sometimes conflicting from others who visited describing the architectural achievements, through to the destructions and what is left remaining.

Hanging Gardens of Babylon

600BC

When the reign of Babylon passed father to son, Nebuchadnezzar II the new ruler, launched a military campaign across Iraq building his new empire. Returning home from a successful conquest his army brought riches along with a queen who Nebuchadnezzar had met during the conquest. In Babylon she was discontent, missing the mountains of her home and the forests which grew all around, her new home now flat and dry. As a gift Nebuchadnezzar constructed a large series of balconies, held up by stone columns reaching up twenty meters in the centre of his city. With this large construction a new device had to be invented for irrigation to bring water to the top balcony where it could run down each layer. Using rotating screw water is drawn upwards which could water the many aromatic plants and trees planted on the balconies, they hung over the edges of terraces looking like a mountainous forest bringing plenty of shade.

There are no accounts from any Greek seeing the gardens for themselves, but sources are taken from others describing them at an earlier date. Gardens were not a new creation; they had been made for those rich enough to afford the privilege to build and maintain them. The construction at Babylon being far bigger than any other in the world.

Historical accounts left by Nebuchadnezzar, which he left many. Neither keep record of its construction or existence. After his conquest there were many approved large structures to be built detailed records remain. Somehow the largest and presumably most important construction of the gardens do not appear, neither is it mentioned in affiliation with Nebuchadnezzar at any time. The story centres around him coming from Greeks sources, the whole meaning behind the construction was attributed to be an extravagant gift for his wife, which equally has no record of ever marrying. Following his death in 562BC writings of the gardens do not appear until three hundred years later, which questions if they ever did exist.

When archaeologists first uncovered Babylon an archway was found with deep wells in the city. Being right by the Palace it was naturally assumed to be the entrance to the gardens, supplied from the wells, its advanced irrigation being a later addition to the story. Being located right next to the palace to would have been the exact site described. It did not prove to be the gardens, instead disappointingly a collection of storage buildings.

It was more recently realized Babylon does not have enough rainfall to support the luxury of such a garden, it would need to be almost entirely supplied from a huge source of water continually running. Water would need to be in far for abundance than they could spare from the Euphrates River. Leading towards the gardens never did exist, which made sense as no one directly saw it, at the very least the enormity of it could not have been as described, it would have needed to be far smaller if one were to exist inside the walls of Babylon, turning it story to myth.

698BC

Before the time of Nebuchadnezzar, the Assyrian capital Ninover had become advanced society. They had built aqueducts connecting from the Tigress River, flowing into the city supplying a grand garden, water was transported up by a spinning screw reaching the top of an artificial mountain covered in all sorts of plants, being particularly familiar of how the gardens at Babylon were described. The Assyrians went on a successful military campaign, they took Babylon and ruled it for a time. On entry to the conquered city its magnificence inspired taking its name and giving it to their own capital, as well as adopting several street names for Ninover. A hundred years later the father of Nebuchadnezzar II, fought back claiming independence for Babylon.

331BC

After the conquest of Alexander the Great reached Ninover, they had been the ones to have seen the gardens, in place being referred to as Babylon. Having an advanced irrigation system inside the city as described by Greek sources to Babylon. The location of the gardens became mixed up from transferring the name from the blue walled city to Ninover. Being referred to as their location, the majority of the army were unaware of the history, which hid the location of the gardens. Depictions of what Ninover actually look like shows an aqueduct arriving to the city, covered on top by trees and falling over a hillside supplying the trees and plants with water around the palace, not necessarily a screw device. The rest of the story of the screw, location and back story later being fantasised around Nebuchadnezzar, which explains why the gardens were not found in Babylon itself and not kept on record by them.

Temple Of Artemis

700BC

There is a long history of building at the city of Ephesus, first having a temple built from a bronze age society, the original wooden structure was destroyed by flooding. Later over the foundation a new temple was to be built. Using animals to help carry blocks of white marble from the quarry to its site the new temple was built, larger than the first.

553BC

The second construction had made the largest temple in the world, taking 10 years to build. The end of the second temple is associated with a man named Herostratus, hoping to solidify him name as the man who destroyed the temple and gain eternal fame. He started a fire on the wooden beams holding up the top of the roof, managing to evade all guards in the process. The fire caught damaging the structure.

The fire happened on the day Alexander the Great was born, it was said afterwards the god Artemis had his back to the temple that day, overseeing the birth of Alexander which allowed his temple to be destroyed. Other reports account for the temple being destroyed by fire, but not explicitly stating its cause was deliberate, possibly resulting from damage following a lightning storm. A nameless fire is coherent with one Greek starting it, following his crime the arsonists name was forbidden to be spoken, voiding him of the fame he desired and was sentenced to death.

There may not have been any arsonist in the first place, the temple had begun sinking into the ground. It was never going to be maintained and its days were always numbered. Public opinion would not be in favour to have the temple deconstructed and rebuilt elsewhere, being it was an attraction. So a conspiracy from the priests may have formed, if they themselves caused enough structural damage they could justify repairing it and moving it to a better location with more stable ground. Following the fire whether it was a conspiracy or one man's selfish desire for fame, reconstruction was denied and the total damage from the fire is unknown but may have been minor as the temple was still in use.

Alexander arrived once he had grown, hearing the news of its damage once he had finished his campaign. He offered to pay for reconstruction, but this was refused as it would not have been proper for one God to build a temple dedicated to another god, they elected to fund repairs themselves. It was finally reconstructed once funds had been saved 20 years later for the third and final time. It was built to be the largest of those which came before it, which were already huge. Outside the temple was decoratively painted and had stone statues on the rood. The inside filled with artworks, sculptures and parts covered in gold.

196BC

The city was fought over by invading Egyptian armies, then taken by the Romans. In the centuries of roman occupation until 30AD, Christianity rose throughout Europe. Ephesus still was busy with trade and visits to see the grand temple. It was soon closed as it depicted a pagan god by the fast-spreading Christianity. A few hundred years after, invading Germanic tribes took the city and finished burning down the internal wooden supports. It is unknown just how much damaged it received by the second fire. Again it went without any repairs as it was not worth the resources to restore a pagan temple. It was again reopened for a short time after its second fire but soon closed. It was dismantled the stone being repurposed for other buildings.

Statue Of Zeus

456BC

Being at the top of the Greek gods, Zeus was bound to receive dominating portrayals worthy of his stature. Most grand of all, the centre piece statue dedicated to him at temple of Olympia. It was built specifically to house this grand statue; it was to be the gods resting place on earth. Before this temple was built, a previous tribute to Zeus was a sacrificial mound. Made from animals sacrificed then burnt to ash, their ashes were mixed with water and added to the mound, it grew over time to be a large mound, which is still scattered over the remaining site today. The temple of Zeus would have been ideally suited by this mound at the front of its entrance. An already existing temple was built there so instead chose its site to be close by next to the other temple. It was funded by the spoils taken after a military campaign. It took 14 years to build the particularly large temple. It was painted inside and out with bright colours, showing images of Zeus and other carved sculptures of mythological scenes. On the roof was centaurs and figures decorating the outside.

The statue of Zeus was created in a workshop nearby, it took over 12 years to finish, all being hand sculpted. It began with a wooden framework with its exterior shaped and attached. The skin shown on Zeus' legs, arms, torso, and face were made using thin sheets of ivory. It had never been worked this way before, it had to be peeled thin but still remain workable which required a new technique to produce it this way. It was found by heating it and soaking in vinegar, the ivory would soften enough to be shaped and pliable to the statue.

His throne was ornamented with gold plates. Decorated with ebony and ivory, finished with inlayed precious stones. Across its panels were depictions of mythological scenes and gods, the exact images were never copied. Around the legendary structure was a shallow pool of oil, used for keeping people back to preserving the statue but also it was needed as oil had to be applied to the ivory for preserving it.

Once completed it was brought in pieces, to be assembled in the temple. Being permitted inside was not an everyday occurrence, it was not a regular church but was a god's house, visited by those wealthy or making a sacrifice could be granted entry. Inside would have been dark, lit from glowing torches hung round the inside walls. The flames would light up the golden throne making it glow. Emerging from the darkness the grand statue sitting on his throne dominating the room, nearly reaching the height of the sealing.

It was taken from Olympia to Rome by emperor Caligula, he wanted to seize many notable statues to have their heads removed, to add a likeness of himself and be seen as a god. Fortunately, he died within the year, even before the statue of Zeus had arrived. It was then sold and taken to Constantinople where it remained for hundreds of years before it burned during a fire and destroyed in 450AD.

Olympia today has recovered some preserved coins from the time the statue stood. Depicting its image from side on. It is almost tall as the roof like descriptions state. Across its depictions they do differ slightly, possibly being repaired the statue changed over time. If not being described differently, leading to differences in artistic depictions put on coins. It is pictured with Zeus being sat on his throne, holding in his left hand a wooden sceptre or a spear. In his right hand is either a bird or an angelic figure, being symbolic of a victory goddess. The differing objects being held by him could have been replaced, leading to the contrasting depictions. Some features did remain constant, he is always bearded and wearing a crown of olives. The original workshop site has been found revealing traces of scrap ivory and precious stones, proving it was the workshop which still has materials such as moulds used for the original.

Lighthouse Of Alexandria

323BC

During the life of Alexander the Great, he carved himself out a huge empire. Producing no heir to follow his succession his death left the empire unstable. Following the void in power Alexanders achievement broke apart. After his death control was fought for between his generals.

Ptolemy founded Alexandria after claiming kingship of Egypt for himself, named after his former commander Alexander. The site was chosen as a trading port, in front of its coast there was an island called Pharos with a surrounding reef. Ptolemy commissioned a huge lighthouse be built as part of solidifying his kingship. Lighthouses before its time, had been only a few meters off the ground, only being visible closing in to a harbour. This was about to change, with a megastructure towering at 130 meters by completion. It was one of the tallest buildings in the world after its 12-year construction was completed by Ptolemy's son, as he had died during its works. It made Alexandria of great importance with such an impressive structure.

Underwater exploration has found over forty ships have sunk around the harbour of Alexandria, being a particularly dangerous bit of reef, the lighthouse was needed for the port to grow. The people living on Pharos, before the lighthouse was built were said to have lured ships to the rocks, wrecking their ships and looting its cargo. The remains found of ships sinking around the reef are not all from being sunk on to or on Pharos but generally its waters. Luring ships and retrieving goods from underwater would be extremely dangerous, there is no doubt been several ships to be damaged and wrecked on Pharos which could have been looted but an overall scheme luring ships became part of the story. The large number of wrecks around the port could also be accounted for the sea being particularly busy, naturally resulting in more wrecks, especially with a dangerous high reef would not help those unfamiliar. The lighthouse was a necessity for Alexandria to become a more dominant city in Egypt.

Built on the outside using white granite and marble to reflect the outside from the sun. Limestone, sandstone, and pink granite lined the inside. Construction had built three levels, the bottom being a 30-meter rectangular base and two circular levels on top reaching its peak. Each level had multiple rooms inside with a spiralling staircase throughout leading to the top. During the day, the highest section had a bronze reflective dish to signal ships using the sun. Later an addition installed a furnace to be lit at night and seen from forty kilometres away. It is believed to be a later addition as it is not mentioned in earlier accounts but being described much later. At the top of the lighthouse was a statue. Its depiction is not clear, most likely it was Poseidon if not Alexander or Ptolemy himself.

After its completion, now being able to navigate ships in its harbour. Alexandria seen a huge boom in trade and tourism making the city very wealthy. Ptolemy had created a three-hundred-year reign for himself and his descendants. They expanded the city and built the library of Alexandria, housing the biggest collection of knowledge from antiquity, keeping around forty thousand scrolls containing a huge record of written knowledge. During the reign of Julius Cesar, during a retreat from the city he ordered the ships in the harbour be torched to allow his escape. The fire spread from the harbour across much of the city destroying it, above all burning down the library, possibly the world's greatest achievement above all construction work lost. The lighthouse eventually fell into Roman and Persian possession following the reign of Ptolemy's descendants.

The area is prone to seismic activity, the lighthouse managed to make it through multiple earthquakes over its time standing. First hit in 796AD not causing too much damage, there was then increasing concerning after cracks formed from more damage in 951AD. It was hit again by earthquakes five years later, when twenty meters of tower collapsed during its time in Islamic control. They rebuilt the top and replaced it with a dome which is their style of building.

Further eruptions under the Mediterranean created a tsunami which hit Alexandria again resulting in structural damage. The last earthquake crumbled the tower in 1323AD only leaving a tiny section remaining standing. By 1480AD the ruin was repurposed, they reclaimed what they could. The threat of religious wars was still ongoing, so from the ruins of the lighthouse were converted into a fortress and bringing in new material to finish it. The fortress still remains today, and the rest of the lighthouse lays below the sea.

Colossus Of Rhodes

305BC

Between the Mediterranean and Aegean is the island of Rhodes, its fabled with tales of a native a population of female warriors called Amazonians. Old grave sites on the island have a lot of female bodies sustaining a lot of damage from weapons. A considerably higher amount than what was expected, proving there was at one time a force of female fighters. The island was settled by the Greeks becoming an important port city state, home to the sun god Helios.

After Alexander died, Rhodes was a huge player in controlling sea trade, being situated in a powerful position its wealth grew. An alliance was made with Ptolemy of Egypt, Rhodes having a large fleet and being an ally with Alexandria was seen a huge threat by Alexandria's rival Macedonia. They decided to take Rhodes before it could ally itself militarily with Alexandria.

They sent a fleet of 40,000 men to attack, they split their force taking their ships to surround the port setting up a blockade. They did not have enough ships to take the port, a blockade was enough to achieve their goals of preventing bringing supplies to Rhodes as the other half of their force sieged the city by land. Rhodes had fortifications, but with only seven thousand men to protect themselves, holding out was going to be a tough fight.

As they kept behind their walls the countryside was taken first, looting and destroying everything not safe behind walls. Attacks by the Macedonians to take the walls seemed promising at first, they managed to get men over, but they were all soon enough killed without being able to hold the walls long enough to breach them and push into the city.

Huge siege towers and rams were then constructed to help capture the walls. They built the largest siege tower ever made at 40 meters high and weighing 160 tonnes. It was coated in iron to prevent it from being burned down, inside it had sixteen internal catapults to defend it as it would be pushed to the walls. It did not work; it took hundreds of men to push the tower up to the walls. On the way the tower suffered enough damage to the iron coating, it left the wood vulnerable to be destroyed and was pulled back not to risk it. Before the attack word was sent to Alexandria for help, their ally needed to quickly pull together a force and sail to their aid making a quick arrival. The Macedon's had no choice but to return to their ships and sail away, leaving behind a lot of their armour, weapons, and shields along with the siege tower. Their possessions were seized and melted down to make an icon marking the great victory.

292BC

A bronze statue of Helios was to be built commending the victory. It was finished after 12 years of work; it was moved to be positioned at the entrance to the port. It was put on to a pedestal and reached thirty meters high. The statue was supported internally with an iron framework, the outside was covered in cast bronze plates attached to the iron frame. Once finished it was named the Colossus, a new word needed to be invented to describe such a huge statue, it became a landmark to those visiting Rhodes, often coming just to see it.

The stance of the statue is unknown with sources offering differing descriptions. Other statues depicting Helios show him holding an arm up to block out the sun from his eyes, which would be a typical stance for a sun god. Being associated with a military defeat a more appropriate pose for its occasion could have been used. Medieval accounts depict the statue as standing one leg each on a pedestal either side of the port entrance. Being a particularly dominating statue, this fantasied image could not have been standing like this, the size would have to have been many times bigger and beyond construction capability. It is considered to have realistically stood on a single pedestal much like New York's statue of Liberty which was later inspired by it.

Cited next to the harbours entrance or on an island near the harbours.

226BC

A few decades after its construction the entire top section collapsed, after an earthquake broke it at the knees. The statue fell into large pieces which scattered over the ground. Alexandria again came to the aid of Rhodes, offering to help pay to fix the Colossus. Instead an oracle was consulted about making repairs, which was refused so its pieces were left where they lay. This did not stop it from still being an attraction, what still lay still had its appeal to keep visitors coming to see its huge broken pieces. Most of the visitors before its collapse would have not been able to read the accounts for the time it stood. Possibly making the confusion related to its stance, there was a considerably longer period the statue lay broken, those visiting it would have imagined the pieces fitting together. Creating different ideas of what they thought it would have looked like, confusing the original positioning.

653

While under Muslim control the statue was decided to be further dismantled, to be shipped back to the mainland and sold. It took nine hundred camels to carry away the entire statue leaving nothing behind.

Mausoleum at Halicarnassus

351BC

The ruler of Halicarnassus, Mausolus commissioned a large tomb to be built from white marble, for himself and his wife. Grand structures would take over a decade to be built, with life being considerably shorter then and with political instability leading to a lot of wars and little to no effective healthcare. Large tombs had to be constructed early on in a ruler's life to be completed before it would be needed. After all the next rulers would not be as inclined to continue making such an expenditure when not required. After the first year of construction Mausolus had died and the project was overseen by his wife.

It was rectangular with three levels of construction built onto one another, each layer covered with dozens of statues depicting his family members and gods. All crafted by the best sculptors of the time. The top layer had thirty-six columns built to support the roof, with steps leading up to the top where a four horsed chariot was positioned, carrying Mausolus and his wife. It was incredibly rare for the time to have a woman seen riding a chariot, the feature may have been part of an incredibly forward-thinking society to have a woman on a chariot. Or made as an addition by his wife, overseeing and paying for the structure following her husband's death. The large structure was the first of its kind named the Mausoleum after its first commission.

Underneath its base are tunnels, leading to chambers where the bodies are kept. Along with possessions and treasures, which were all sealed. Preventing them from being looted and the large scale of this tomb becoming an attraction. At some point before its destruction looters had bought the house closest to the temple. They brought in tunnelling equipment to make a secret dig, creating a shaft which still exists where drills were used to remove the earth and tunnel through to the temple. Inside the burial room, they found a huge sarcophagus, it was far larger than what was needed signifying the importance of the man for whom it was built. It stood until the thirteenth century when it had collapsed by an earthquake, the rock was left piled where it fell and was later used by crusaders to build their fortifications.

Easter Island

Remote in the South Pacific of Chile there is a partially small island, it is sixty-three square miles of grass hills and plains. Formed from its volcanic crater leaving behind the rocky outcrop it now is. The finest of its rock has been ground after millions of years weathering into sand, making its way down by the bay area's, forming beaches by the coasts. The land hosted plant life, fish in its reefs and allowed birds to settle.

300 – 1300

Voyagers had eventually made it to the island and decided to stay, making it theirs. They are genetically related to Polynesians, who were a sea faring people travelling and making colonies all over islands across the Pacific. This particular group became involved in a tribal war when they chose to escape. Fleeing on canoes, far off to a new land, they travelled around two thousand miles away, taking around 19 days before reaching the island. They may have already known of it having been discovered previously. It is so remote large supplies of food would be needed to have made the long voyage to come across it, Polynesians occupied around the north Pacific where Easter island is in the south.

It is unknown when they exactly arrived, they had the capability for a long time to reach it but may have found it much later. For their culture to have developed with the traditions they had, it is assumed they at least inhabited the land, between the middle of an early and late habitation, around 1200AD. They had made it to a new home and are named the Rapa Nui on Easter Island.

They burnt down heavily covered woodland, clearing space for crops to be grown and fishing vessels constructed. Over hundreds of years after their arrival, there is likely to have been a secondary wave of travellers having found their way and stayed, or at least had made contact and traded with Polynesians. They were sailing further west and could have found South America, sweet potatoes have been farmed on Easter Island, native to the South of America. The only source of writing found on the island exists on the rongorongo tablet, featuring many organised hieroglyphic symbols. It is not understood, being its only source of this language, it resembles writing used Lake Titicaca in the Andes. Houses on Easter Island at one point, all had wooden tablets with the same hieroglyphics on the front, naming their ownership.

1300 – 1500

After a few hundred years, they had reached a period of grand building works. Surrounding the inside perimeter of the island, stone statues land in line across the coasts. Built using stone tools, around nine hundred have been found, mainly concentrated around their quarry. Around half have been moved out to the outer perimeter of the island. Named the moai heads, they depict human likenesses, looking internally to the land. Most are made from hardened volcanic ash, reaching up to ten meters high and averaging twenty tonnes. The largest being finished and moved, weighting close to ninety tonnes. larger monoliths had begun construction, the most ambitious nearly doubled the weight, it was never finished and left abandoned as it was far too heavy to be moved, it was left still attached to the ground in the quarry.

If there was any period integral to the completion and moving of the stone. Significant times all over the ancient world, guide their megalithic positioning with the rising sun of the summer and winter solstice. With meaning considered throughout major construction sites of the ancient world, most cultures were familiar with the celebration of the solstice, which could have been an ideal time to have them finished and moved in place, making their own culture they equally could attribute their own meanings and completed them whenever they had enough time and people to be able to do so.

What was originally found just the heads, they were thought to be the entire structure, but a number have now been dug up to show the full bodies. Which features a torso, limbs, and clothing, they have carvings covering their backs. These markings are not fully understood, they could be tattooed images or depictions of tools used for farming and daily life as some resemble canoes. The monoliths have bodies buried underneath the ground, by placing them this way their buried waist would hold them in place and still display the details of their torso and heads. They have been covered over by earth after the centuries of sitting there leaving only the heads visible. Their weight not helping them either as they are sinking into the ground at the same time as being slowly covered over. Fortunately, by remaining buried it helped preserve them, keeping them from the weathering. Features remaining above ground are so well defined and exaggerated, they have remained preserved.

They were finished with emphasises features, being very dominating to their characteristics which they all share. They have large heads with large square jaw lines, elongated ears, and noses with large lips. Under the ground, excavations found thick torsos with arms laying in different positions, either by the side or across the body. There are no legs they curve round making the base but have carved loin cloths. They were finished being polished, rubbing soft pumice against the surface and covered with decorations adding colour to the eyes, some even being painted red a sacred colour. Later works added carved red headdresses to more important figures, they were placed dry on top most of which have since fallen.

They may have functioned purely symbolically as likenesses of former chiefs and powerful individuals, being memorializing them after death but not directly serving as grave sites. They had a belief system which granted the dead great power over the lives of the living, providing health and fortune for their harvests, which would require offerings. Working with wood and stone to prepare these megalithic stone works, give spiritual power called mana to the stone, it is stored in the statue's hair. Larger and heavier constructions naturally being of more importance and requiring more work, contain more of these spiritual properties.

Serving as religious projects, they could have just been aesthetic in nature. Their construction banding together communities living on the island, sharing a single culture. Building them could provide contest between their construction. The largest being of more prestige, giving more power to their builders, bringing them better luck with it looking over them. Their positioning provides a surprizing vital function than first realized, or even intended. Soil erosion on the island is an ongoing issue, being so exposed to coastal weather and being so small an island, living their permanently would be challenging. The weight of large stones placed around the perimeter acts as a barrier keeping soil inland. Most of the inland soil is low in nutrients, the best farmland is by the coast. By heaving the large head they may have been a symbol of luck, looking over crops. Even identifying who they belong too. It may have been a conscious realization or not, but they did function to improve their farm land, many were placed right where they are needed for this purpose.

Living space was created by constructing stone houses. Piling walls of small rocks, these buildings were passed down generationally. Staying on such a small island permitted an excess of time to develop culture. They based religious beliefs around shamanism and lived across a few separate settlements, all still sharing the same beliefs. To the edge by the coast, a large cave under rocky cliff edges has depictions of daily life activities in rock paintings. They show people fishing, the birds living on the mainland as well as the surrounding rocks offshore. Each year the tribes would come together to host an annual contest. Each tribe living from their own villages would put forward a competitor to become the islands champion for their version of a triathlon. They would enter a particularly dangerous race, the course would take them running up the rocky cliffs, down the other side to the shore, a swim across the ocean to the nearby island that homed the rarest birds. They would take an egg and swim it back, finishing the race would be the first back to the waiting tribe members and hailed as the victor. Rewarded for risking their lives they would live in luxury, staying in a large stone house for the next year, until the following race.

Culture seems to be shared at some point, between the two cultures of Polynesians and South Americans. Pottery and weaving skills are of similar craftsmanship. Famously in the South American cultures are their huge workings of stone. Deciding to take on such a difficult and demanding task is shared between the two, South America has huge walls, pyramids and temples built of stone. Most relatable to the Moai heads are the giant Olmec heads, being the only remaining remanets of a lost culture. Further huge works using stone have been undertaken to a large degree of success, all over the world. Possible being a huge coincidence the practice is shared, equally that of a considerably more complexed society who were in contact with each all across the world, sharing ideas and travelling before the knowledge was forgotten. Moai heads are not considered to be a direct copy of South American cultures stone work, or the Olmec heads as they have a full body and are made with their own aesthetic style, but South American work could have inspired the development of their own practices to create their leaders, ancestors, or deities to look over them and protect the land.

European Arrival

1772

Life for the secluded population, could not remain eternally hidden during colonisation. It was eventually found by Europeans on Easter morning, giving the island its name. On arrival they met a local population of around three thousand which were spread out, all over the land in their own groups. Amazed by the huge heads surrounding the place, they found the primary source of stone was coming from a single quarry site. The other red stone used for the head dresses were coming from different quarry site. They had no clue to how they were moved all over the island.

The original method of transport will never be exactly known. They are long thought to be the work of log rollers and brute force. To move the larger monoliths using strength alone, would have been a huge task to undertake, using such a crude method does not seem possible. The land is particularly uneven throughout. Without any large mammals to help pull the stone and without having invented the wheel, it appears a mystery to how it was achieved.

No one has seen for themselves how they done it. When travellers were able to communicate with the Rapa Nui, as they share a language remarkably like French Polynesian. They were told a rather mythical story of the stones walking themselves across the island, from the quarry to their final resting place. At first, this vague translation serves to tell they either had no clue themselves, with the monoliths being far older than their history knew, or by their own interpretation they had indeed told the truth and the multiple tonne stones had walked.

Experimental archaeology on the island has assessed one method of moving a rock across the island, they used a relatively small, four tonne rock to assess their method with around a dozen people and were successful. By wrapping long vines around the upper sections of the statues, when they split between two teams each at either side of the stone, they could pull on the vines and begin to rock it back and forth. Both teams working together would build up momentum. When they position themselves slightly in front of the rock, it its pulled forwards towards them. The view of any onlooker would be an upright carved rock, walking as it swings from left to right moving slowly into its intended position.

The stone moved was achieved by an exceedingly small number of people, moving a considerably smaller monolith compared to that of the largest. Moving considerably larger stones would require even with more people, proportionate to its size. Moving a considerably larger stone would still have its own challenges. Vines would need to be thicker to avoid snapping and toppling the stone over, which would risk all the work to make it if it cracks. Land would have to be at a more gradual incline to move larger stones up higher elevations. Most efficiently the stones could have been quarried in the rough shape it would need to be, it would reduce as much weight as possible from the rock making it as easy as possible to move, it could be taken in its unfinished forum to the site where it would have its details carved on the backs, arms, and heads.

Unfinished moai still stay in their quarry, they are found to have a finished level of detail made on their faces and bodies while the rock is still attached to the quarry, so were nearly finished before being moved, they must have been confident they could move it carefully enough. They were then needed to be lifted upright, most easily achieved through pulling it rather than pushing, using leverage to help wedge them up and keeping them in place by sticking log under it as it is lifted. Finally vines attached at a high point around the neck where it was walked to its resting place for the final carving, polishing, and decorating.

The quiet island life for the Rapa Nui ended abruptly. The final days of the culture has been disputed as the inhabitants mostly vanished, following the first recorded contact. When the island was first inhabited it was covered in trees, some of which had to be cleared to free up land and to be used in building fishing vessels, burnt for light and warmth at night, used for cooking and all other purposes of construction. Being confined to a relatively small area, all natural resources were vital and would have to be expertly managed to ensure their renewal for long term survival. Over centuries of inhabitancy, it was long believed generations depleted trees before they had time to regrow which led to heavy soil erosion at a much faster rate than expected, as roots binding the soil together holding in its nutrients were lost, no longer keeping it from being washed into the ocean. The loss of fertile soil would be devastating for farming, which is holding up a community reliant on the soils to sustain themselves. New food sources would have to be used to supplement failing harvest, the fish and bird populations would be the next available source of food, leading to their overall decline as well.

Living between nine separated tribes, now with reduced resources and nearing their end, could see an increase in competition between groups. Possibly encouraging faster depletion of wood, by trying to store it for themselves rather than otherwise leave it. When the last tree was cut and used, they would not have been unable to regrow more if seeds not saved, equally a tree would require decades to be fully regrown. Without any more wood they would be stuck, unable to sail away. Possibly techniques and knowledge from their ancestors, voyaging hundreds of years before became lost. With failing harvests and at the height of their population, size would quickly collapse through starvation or through ensuing civil wars.

Evidence shows few bodies have been found, showing they died from wounds received from weapons relevant to a war. Most signs of injuries have attempted to have been healed. When Europeans arrived, they found the natives to be wielding obsidian weapons, using short spears, and longer throwing javelins, a favourite of south American cultures. They were thought to be purely as weapons for war against other tribes, as they were no big mammals to hunt. Civil war was considered responsible for population destruction, though few of these weapons were ever found. Having so few examples found on the island, shows they could be weapons but equally tools used for their sharp edges in daily tasks use like preparing food. They also had wooden clubs and stone throwing slings, used for sport or in celebrations providing activities for entertainment. In times of war, everyone would be required for the duty of protecting their home. They the few weapons they had access too, but to what capacity they were trained either used recreational or being dedicated to their training is not clear. Evidence generally shows there was no large-scale fights between groups in a civil war, as it would result with many killed and wounded, which is not what is found. They had no coherent standing military or army as such, fighting was not a part of a coherent army but from individual skills to protect themselves.

The population may have not been in any decline before European arrival. Only being home to a maximum of three thousand people. It was assumed it must have once homed far more people to be capable of building such large stone works. The islands maximum capacity is estimated to be up to over seventeen thousand people, considerably larger to what they had. So assumed a larger population must have existed at some point to be able to complete the stone works. Then the destruction of trees leads to a decline of population back down to around three thousand.

Their stone working custom took place over most of its roughly five-hundred-year inhabitancy, beginning soon after the first arrival of people. It served to use the abundance of time, as they do not need to travel far or build new homes but still needed to be banded together with shared tradition. The works could be achieved continually, requiring much less effort than believed. Only producing and moving two Moai per year, to achieve what they had by the end. The practice passed down from generation to the next, continuing all the way until the end was nearing when they stopped producing these megaliths.

1862

Later external pressures came with the arrival of Peruvian ships. They raided the island during the peak of the slave trade and seen the natives as an easy target being confined. Slave ships took half the population including their leader, his son and all their religious priests, removing all those versed in native tradition. The way of life could no longer be passed down or maintained by the other half of the population left behind. Not that their troubles were over, they were left diseases which devastated those remaining. Following the absence of leadership, social control broke down and subjected the people to chaos. Warriors came out on top, being the strongest and most feared individuals leading to destruction of their own settlements.

Of those who were taken and made the sea voyage to Peru, ninety percent had died within the first year of capture through work and disease. The capture was among the last trips made of the slave trade, capturing native peoples was abolished three years later. Few survivors made it over the years of hardship, those not among the majority dying in the first year had further losses over the next two. They were finally rounded up to be sent back to their island.

During their voyage back, once again disaster struck. There was a smallpox outbreak onboard ship, being confined put everyone to be at risk of catching the disease, even fewer survived the journey home. Only fifteen made it back of the fifteen hundred taken, who brought smallpox back with them to spread it the rest who had stayed there. Without their leaders and few still living on the island, they only had a population around a hundred still alive. It is still possible to come back from such devastation, over time rebuilding but once again disaster came to those few still living. Not only were resources still in short supply and suffering from erosion. The travels by all those visitors who made it to Easter Island had unintentionally brought with them, Polynesian rats who had stowed away on ships and escaped to the island. They were highly destructive to the environment, eating tree saplings which halted the rejuvenation of resources and prevented all the benefits of a renewable resource, making life even harder.

Nearing the end of island life, those few remaining toppled their Moai statues. Thought to be as a result of in fighting or possibly made as a final effort to keep as much weight spread across the ground to stop the severe erosion now being accelerated by the rats. Toppling them could be a sign of casting away their old beliefs, which had failed them. They destroyed the mana held within them and marked a change in their spiritual beliefs.

From the disease and slave trade which decimated the population, considerably reduced resources, and arrival of destructive invasive species, would all together be the tipping point past rebuilding for the Rapa Nui. Native people were able to last so long with careful management of resources and keep a limited population to maintain balance. Even with some troubles of erosion, would be surely realized the threat and protected themselves against it, the same as many other people adapting to their environment. The change they could not adapt to was colonisation, being targeted living in such a small place would prevent a means to escape, those who remained had the fallout from diseases, of which they had little to no immunity. The culture and knowledge they had could have taught the world about themselves and what they have achieved. Instead the cultural value was not considered at this time and were instead enslaved or killed for personal profit, leaving the islands baron with later Europeans travelling back to the island. No survivors remained to be looked over by the Moai. They are left to continually sink further into the ground, out of existence just as their creators did.

About the Author

Living in Scotland surrounded by history had peaked an interest for over a decade now. What started out as a story book for kids, developed over the last five years into the Mythic Codex Volume one. Learning history, starting out as a hobby made, me realize the value of extending general knowledge that most people are familiar with, to a far better understanding of the history behind these stories after many hours of research. Dedicating so much time for research can be difficult, which is why I have put together the first part to a collection of historically based mysteries and treasures.

Printed in Great Britain
by Amazon